ABOUT TI

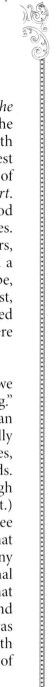

We are excited to introduce the second official *When Calls the Heart* - Cookbook "Another Heartie Helping". This follows the first official *When Calls the Heart* cookbook release "Dining with the Hearties." We set out to gather the best recipes from the best fans ever – The Hearties. The Hearties, numbering in the tens of thousands, are fans of the television show, *When Calls the Heart*. Through videos and promotions, we asked them, over a period of months, to submit their best "go to, no miss" meals and dishes. From those recipes we selected a variety of breads, appetizers, side dishes, salads, main dishes and desserts. We then hired a professional chef and proceeded to cook every single recipe, photograph and test it. We selected the dishes we liked best, and assembled the cookbook. The response we received was incredible and people were asking when we were going to do it again.

Well, we have! We repeated the process and we can now offer you "Another Heartie Helping." And the recipes are just as fantastic. We can say that with assurance as we personally tested every single dish, sometimes, asking for seconds and even thirds. We're that committed. (A very tough job, one that we were anxious to repeat.) Every full color picture that you see was made from the exact recipe that you see next to it. Like before, many of the recipes also have personal notes and testimonials about what the food meant to that person and their families. This cookbook was put together with loving care with you in mind, the wonderful fans of *When Calls the Heart.*

TABLE OF CONTENTS

BREADS
ANOTHER HEARTIE HELPING

CARAMEL ORANGE RING

Submitted by: Lori Pearson

Prep time	Cook time	Serves
15 min	**40 min**	**10-12**

- 1 tablespoon butter, softened
- ½ cup orange marmalade
- 2 tablespoons pecans, chopped
- 1 cup brown sugar, firmly packed
- ½ teaspoon cinnamon
- 2 (10 oz) cans, biscuits
- ½ cup butter, melted

Preheat oven to 350 degrees. Grease Bundt® pan with softened butter. Place teaspoonfuls of orange marmalade evenly in bottom of pan. Sprinkle with nuts. In small bowl, combine brown sugar and cinnamon.

Mix well and set aside. Separate biscuits and dip them in melted butter then coat them in sugar mixture. Stand biscuits on edge in the pan, on top of the marmalade and nuts, spacing evenly. Sprinkle with remaining sugar mixture and drizzle with remaining melted butter. Bake at 350 degrees for 30 to 40 minutes, until golden brown. Cool in pan for 5 minutes then invert onto serving plate. Serve warm.

CRANBERRY ORANGE BREAD

Submitted by: Luanne Maroney

Prep time **15-20 min**	Cook time **55-60 min**	Serves **2 loaves**

ingredients

- 1 cup butter, softened (not melted)
- 1 ¾ cup granulated pure cane sugar
- 2 tablespoons orange zest
- 3 eggs
- ½ teaspoon vanilla extract
- ¾ cup buttermilk
- 2 ½ cups all-purpose flour
- 2 teaspoons baking powder
- 1 teaspoon salt
- 2 ½ cups fresh or dried cranberries

Orange Glaze:
- 1 ½ cups powdered sugar
- 1 tablespoon orange juice
- 1 tablespoon orange zest
- 1 tablespoon milk
- 1 teaspoon vanilla extract

instructions

Preheat oven to 350 degrees. In large mixing bowl, cream butter, sugar and orange zest together for 3 to 5 minutes. Add eggs one at a time and beat 1 minute per egg. Then add vanilla. In separate bowl, mix dry ingredients. Add dry ingredients to wet mix, alternating with buttermilk until well mixed. Then fold in cranberries. Grease and flour two regular size loaf pans and divide batter into two pans. Bake at 350 degrees for 55 to 60 minutes until a toothpick comes clean when checking. Let loaves cool completely before adding the glaze. For glaze: mix powdered sugar and orange zest with milk, orange juice and vanilla until creamy. Drizzle glaze over loaves after they have cooled on rack.

notes

This is a very tasty and moist bread. It is great by itself for a snack or as a breakfast bread. I love having it for company during holidays for brunch or taking it to friends as a gift (and that's usually the best time for finding fresh cranberries in the grocery store). It can be frozen and saved for later. Just add the glaze after thawing to serve.

LEMON BLUEBERRY BANANA BREAD

Submitted by: Lindsey Stephens

Prep time	Cook time	Serves
20 min	1 hour and 10 min	6-8

- 1 cup white sugar
- ½ cup butter, softened
- 1 teaspoon vanilla or lemon extract
- 4 bananas, mashed
- ½ cup milk
- 3 eggs
- 2 cups flour
- 1 teaspoon baking soda
- ½ teaspoon salt
- ¼ teaspoon cream of tartar
- ¾ cup fresh blueberries
- 1 to 2 tablespoons lemon zest

Preheat oven to 350 degrees. In a large bowl, mix together sugar and butter. Add extract, bananas, milk, and eggs. Then add flour, baking soda, salt, and cream of tartar.

Fold in lemon zest and blueberries. Bake for 1 hour and 10 minutes or until a toothpick inserted in the center comes out clean.

I created this recipe by accident when I was making my original banana bread recipe. I didn't have vanilla, so I used lemon extract instead. I found that adding blueberries and fresh lemon zest made the bread even better! I kept that recipe and now find it the perfect tea time (or any time) snack that Abigail herself would be happy to serve in her café.

CARROT APPLE ZUCCHINI BREAD

Submitted by: Vada S Wilson

Prep time	Cook time	Serves
10-15 min	**50-60 min**	**24**

- ½ cup unsalted butter, melted
- ½ cup no sugar added cinnamon apple sauce
- 3 eggs
- 1 ½ cups granulated sugar
- ½ cup orange juice
- 1 teaspoon vanilla
- 1 cup carrots, grated
- 1 cup zucchini, grated
- 1 cup apple of choice, grated
- 1 cup pecans, chopped
- 1 cup raisins (may be substituted with 1 cup of grated carrots or zucchini)

- 3 ½ cups all-purpose flour
- ½ teaspoon salt
- 2 ½ teaspoons baking powder
- 1 teaspoon baking soda
- ½ teaspoon cinnamon
- ½ teaspoon pumpkin pie spice

Glaze:
- ½ cup softened cream cheese
- 2 tablespoons softened salt free butter
- 2 ½ to 3 ½ cups powdered sugar
- 1 to 3 tablespoons orange juice as needed to allow icing to drizzle

Preheat oven to 350 degrees. If using raisins, boil 1 cup of raisins in 2 cups of water in a saucepan for 15 minutes; drain and set aside. In a large bowl, combine butter, apple sauce, eggs, orange juice, and vanilla. Once mixed, add carrots, zucchini, apple, pecans and raisins; combine. In a separate bowl, mix together flour, salt, baking soda, baking powder, and spices. Stir (by hand) dry ingredients into carrot, zucchini mixture until all ingredients are combined. Do not over mix, it should <u>not</u> be consistency of cake batter.

Oil and flour two standard loaf pans, add batter, bake for 50-60 minutes or until an inserted toothpick comes out clean. Cool for 10-20 minutes before removing bread from pans.

Glaze: Combine cream cheese, butter, powdered sugar and orange juice as needed. Mix well. Once bread is completely cooled, drizzle glaze over the top.

PUMPKIN SPICE BREAD

Submitted by: Beth Pranke

Prep time	Cook time	Serves
10 min	**1 hour + cooling**	**2 loaves**

- 3 cups sugar
- 1 cup vegetable oil
- 4 eggs, lightly beaten
- 1 (15 oz) can solid-pack pumpkin
- 3 ½ cups all-purpose flour
- 1 teaspoon baking soda
- 1 teaspoon salt
- 1 teaspoon ground cinnamon
- 1 teaspoon ground nutmeg
- ½ teaspoon baking powder
- ½ teaspoon ground cloves
- ½ teaspoon ground allspice
- ½ cup water

In a large bowl, combine sugar, oil and eggs. Then add pumpkin and mix well. Combine flour, baking soda, salt, cinnamon, nutmeg, baking powder, cloves, allspice and add to pumpkin mixture alternately with water, beating well after each addition. Pour into two greased 9x5 inch loaf pans. Bake at 350 degrees for 60 to 65 minutes or until a toothpick inserted near center comes out clean. Cool in pans 10 minutes before removing and placing on a wire rack to cool completely.

APPLESAUCE OATMEAL MUFFINS

Submitted by: Pat Cory

Prep time	Cook time	Serves
15 min	**20 min**	**12 muffins**

- 1 ½ cup oats
- 1 cup unsweetened applesauce
- 1 ¼ cup flour
- ½ cup skim milk
- ¾ teaspoon cinnamon
- ½ cup brown sugar
- 1 teaspoon baking powder
- 1 tablespoon oil
- ¾ teaspoon baking soda
- 1 egg white

Topping:

- ¼ cup oats
- ⅛ teaspoon cinnamon
- 1 tablespoon brown sugar

Preheat oven to 400 degrees. Combine oats, flour, cinnamon, baking powder and baking soda. Then add applesauce, milk, brown sugar, oil and egg white. Mix until all dry ingredients are moistened. Spoon into greased muffin tin. Combine oats, brown sugar and cinnamon for topping. Sprinkle over muffins. Bake at 400 degrees for 15 to 20 minutes. Makes 1 dozen.

I found this recipe when I was looking for something healthier. It's easy and very tasty. I sometimes add walnuts to the batter, but then I add nuts to almost everything I bake. :)

They are good with or without the topping.

JALAPEÑO CORNBREAD

Submitted by: Azure McDaniel

Prep time	Cook time	Serves
15 min	**30 min**	**12**

- 1 cup self-rising cornmeal
- 2 heaping teaspoons self-rising flour
- 1 egg
- ¼ cup oil
- 1 cup buttermilk
- ½ cup bell pepper, chopped
- 1 cup whole kernel corn
- 1 cup cheddar cheese, grated
- 2 tablespoons jalapeño (for mild or more for heat)

Preheat oven to 450 degrees. In a large bowl, stir together cornmeal, flour, egg, oil and buttermilk; will be soupy.

Then mix in bell pepper, corn, cheese and jalapeño. Pour into greased muffin tin (Either 12 large or 24 mini).

Bake at 450 degrees for 30 minutes.

Enjoy!

FIFTEEN MINUTE CORN PONE

Submitted by: Misty Dawn Ryder

Prep time	Cook time	Serves
15 min	**1 hour**	**10-12**

ingredients

- 3 cups plain cornmeal
- 1 ½ cups plain flour
- 2 cups sugar
- 2 teaspoons baking powder
- 1 teaspoon baking soda
- 1 teaspoon salt
- 2 large eggs
- 1 cup buttermilk
- 2 cups boiling water

instructions

Preheat oven to 400 degrees. Mix cornmeal, flour, sugar and water then let sit for 15 minutes. After fifteen minutes resting period add eggs, salt, baking powder, baking soda, buttermilk and mix until ingredients are well blended. Pour mixture into 2 loaf pans sprayed with your choice of cooking spray. Bake in 400 degree oven for 1 hour.

notes

This recipe can be made with either plain white or plain yellow cornmeal whichever is preferred.

DILLY CASSEROLE BREAD

Submitted by: Laura Dion

Prep time	Cook time	Serves
15 min + 90 min (rise time)	40-50 min	1 Loaf

- 1 packet active dry yeast
- ¼ cup warm water
- 1 cup cottage cheese (warmed to lukewarm)
- 1 tablespoon sugar
- 2 tablespoons instant minced onions
- 1 tablespoon butter
- 2 teaspoons dill seed
- ¼ teaspoon baking soda
- 1 unbeaten egg
- 2 ¼ to 2 ½ cups all-purpose flour
- coarse salt

In a small bowl, mix yeast in ¼ cup warm water. Combine all ingredients, except four, in a large mixing bowl. Gradually add flour to form a stiff dough, beating well after each addition and then cover. Let rise in a warm place until light and double in bulk, 50 to 60 minutes. Press down dough then put into a well-greased 8 inch round cake pan. Let rise in warm place 30 to 40 minutes. Bake at 350 degrees for 40 to 50 minutes until golden brown. Brush with butter and sprinkle with coarse salt.

This was one of my favorite foods at my grandma's house. I loved it so much she taught me how to make it. I now make it for all holidays and family gatherings and the aroma brings back such wonderful memories of time spent with Grandma.

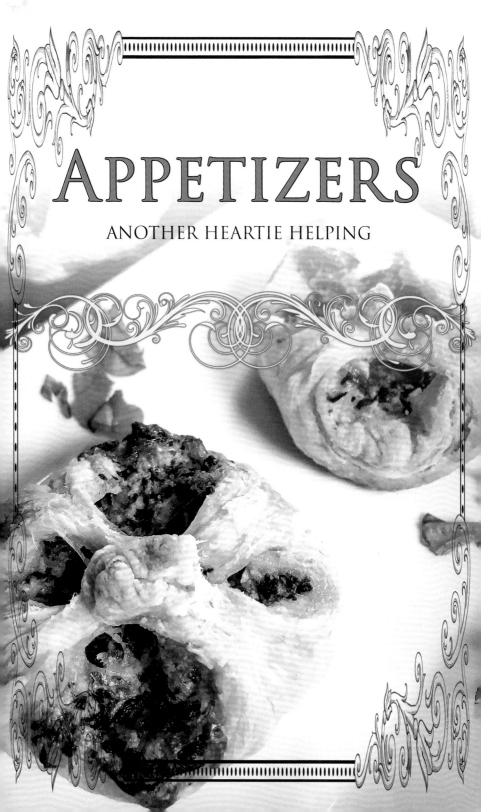

APPETIZERS

ANOTHER HEARTIE HELPING

LAUREYANNES

Submitted by: Laurey Fawcett

Prep time	Cook time	Serves
1 hour	**20-25 min**	**36**

- 1 package frozen chopped spinach
- 2 cups fresh baby spinach leaves
- 1 container smooth ricotta cheese
- 2 cups shredded mozzarella cheese
- 6 mild Italian sausage
- 2 garlic cloves, minced
- 2 teaspoons Louisiana hot sauce
- 4 ounces cream cheese
- 2 boxes President's Choice® brand frozen puff pastry sheets
- salt and pepper to taste

Preheat oven to 400 degrees. Defrost and drain package of frozen chopped spinach, set aside. Squeeze out as much water as possible in a dry dish towel. Brown Italian sausage (casing removed) with garlic, drain oil and set aside to cool. Mix cooled meat and drained spinach with Louisiana hot sauce, ricotta cheese, mozzarella cheese and spinach leaves. Salt and pepper to taste. Cut each puff pastry sheet into 9 squares. Drop a spoonful of filling in the center of each square, gently fold and mold the puff pastry around the filling to seal. Place on parchment paper lined baking sheet and bake in 400 degree oven for 20 to 25 minutes or until golden brown.

Many years ago I ate a spinach and sausage pie and loved the combination of ingredients. I began experimenting with creating something that my kids would love too so it had to have cheese instead of eggs, had to be portable for little hands and needed a crust that didn't make a flaky mess like a pie crust. This was the result. They have become a family favourite that are made for every family get together and now the grandchildren adore them as much as the big kids. I never knew what to call them because spinach, sausage and cheese puffs just seemed too long. I always said I wanted to make a difference in the world, leave some kind of legacy. The kids named them Laureyannes and it just kind of stuck.

SAUERKRAUT-CRANBERRY MEATBALLS

Submitted by: Beth Pranke

Prep time	Cook time	Serves
20-30 min	2 hours	5 dozen meatballs

ingredients

- 2 pounds hamburger
- 1 envelope dry onion soup mix
- 2 large or 3 small eggs
- Roughly 5 ounces Italian bread crumbs

Sauce:
- 14 ounce can sauerkraut, well drained
- ¾ cup brown sugar
- 14 ounce can whole cranberry sauce
- 1 bottle Heinz® Chili Sauce
- 1 bottle water (use chili sauce bottle to measure)

instructions

Preheat oven to 350 degrees. Mix the first 4 ingredients together thoroughly and then roll into small balls (should make 40 to 50). Layer them in a baking pan. Mix the sauce ingredients until dissolved. Pour sauce over the meat and bake at 350 degrees for 1 hour covered and then about 1 hour uncovered. Alternative for Crock-Pot®: Buy a large bag premade meatballs and add to Crock-Pot®. Pour sauce over and simmer for a couple of hours.

HOT
COCOA MIX

Submitted by: Susan Scott

Prep time	Cook time	Serves
5 min	**1 min**	**15 (6 oz) servings**

- 2 cups nonfat dry milk powder
- ¾ cup sugar
- ½ cup cocoa
- ½ cup powdered non-dairy creamer
- dash salt

In mixing bowl, combine all ingredients and blend well. Store in a tightly covered container.

Single serving: combine ¼ cup mix with ¾ cup hot water in cup or mug then stir to blend.

My mother would make this for my sisters and me. It was a special treat with cookies on Christmas Eve.

CHEESE SHRIMP MELT-AWAYS

Submitted by: Sharon Stark

Prep time	Cook time	Serves
25 min	**5 min (broiler)**	**10-12**

- ½ cup butter
- 1 (4 oz) can small deveined shrimp drained
- 1 jar Old English® cheese spread
- 2 packages English muffins (10-12)
- 1 ½ teaspoons mayonnaise
- ½ teaspoon seasoned salt
- ¼ teaspoon garlic powder

Let butter and cheese stand to soften, then mix in medium size bowl. Add shrimp to mixture and blend well. Mix together mayonnaise, garlic powder, and seasoned salt in a separate bowl. Next combine both together and mix well. Spread mixture on halved English muffins. Cut into quarters. Place on cookie sheet and broil until crispy (if time allows freeze for about ½ hour before broiling).

Serve hot.

Makes enough spread for 10-12 english muffins. May be frozen several weeks ahead (after preparing muffins) then broiled from frozen. Great for parties.

MEXICAN CORN DIP

Submitted by: Patty Bird

Prep time	Cook time	Serves
10 min	25-30 min	15-20

- 12 ounces Mexican whole kernel corn, drained
- 2 (4 oz) cans of green chopped chilies, drained
- 1 cup Monterey Jack cheese, shredded
- ½ cup parmesan cheese
- 1 cup mayonnaise
- tortilla chips

Preheat oven to 325 degrees. In a medium bowl, combine all ingredients.

Mix together and spoon into a glass pie plate.

Bake at 325 degrees for 25-30 minutes or until heated through, serve with tortilla chips.

A family favorite!

JEN'S BREAD POT

Submitted by: Debbie Wesselius

Prep time	Cook time	Serves
20 min	90 min	10

ingredients

- 2 cups cheese, grated
- 4 ounces cream cheese
- 1 cup sour cream
- 1 can flakes of ham, diced
- ¼ cup onion, chopped
- 1 teaspoon Worcestershire sauce
- 1 round loaf of bread

instructions

Preheat oven to 300 degrees. Beat all ingredients together except bread. Remove inside of bread after cutting off top. Fill with mixture.

Replace top and wrap loaf in tinfoil. Bake in oven at 300 degrees for 1 ½ hours.

Serve with crackers.

notes

I got this recipe from a friend. It is great for any occasion.

MEXICAN BEAN DIP

Submitted by: Beth Burdick

Prep time	Cook time	Serves
15 min	25 min	one 9x13 pan

- 8 ounces cream cheese
- 8 ounces sour cream
- 1 can refried beans
- 2 to 3 tablespoons taco seasoning
- 8 ounces Colby Jack cheese, shredded

Preheat oven to 350 degrees and spray 9x13 baking pan with cooking spray. In mixer, blend cream cheese, sour cream, beans and taco mix.

Spread evenly in baking pan and sprinkle with cheese. Bake for 25 minutes or until bubbly.

Serve with tortilla chips or over top of a bowl of Fritos®.

REESE'S
SIMPLE SALSA

Submitted by: Reese Chrysler

Prep time	Cook time	Serves
10 min	**none**	**4-6**

ingredients

- 2 cans petite diced tomatoes
- ½ medium onion, chopped
- 3 to 4 jalapeños, finely chopped
- cilantro, finely chopped (optional)
- ½ teaspoon salt
- ½ teaspoon pepper
- ½ teaspoon garlic salt

instructions

In a large bowl, mix together tomatoes, onion and jalapeños.

Next stir in pepper, salt and garlic salt (you can add any of the above ingredients to taste).

Then add finely chopped fresh cilantro (only if you want it). Let it sit for about 20 minutes, stir and enjoy with potato chips or tortilla chips!

notes

Reese changes this recipe often to his taste so you don't have to be accurate on any of it. It's just a fast simple recipe, a go to for a quick salsa!

SAVORY
OYSTER CRACKERS

Submitted by: Beth Burdick

Prep time	Cook time	Serves
15 min	**35 min**	**10-12**

- 12-16 ounces oyster crackers
- ¼ teaspoon lemon pepper seasoning
- 1 teaspoon dill weed
- ¼ teaspoon garlic powder
- ¾ cup oil (olive, canola, vegetable etc)
- 3 tablespoons ranch dressing mix

Preheat oven to 250 degrees. In a large bowl, mix oyster crackers with oil and all seasonings till well covered.

Bake on large foil-lined baking pan at 250 degrees for 20 minutes. Stir or flip crackers over, then bake for 15 to 20 minutes more.

Cool and serve.

Recipe from a family friend, Dana Raines ... and it's ALWAYS a hit at parties and gatherings!!!

Side-Dishes and Salads

ANOTHER HEARTIE HELPING

CHEESY MASHED POTATOES

Submitted by: Christy Spratlin

Prep time 20-30	Cook time 30 min	Serves 10-12

- 5 pounds potatoes, boiled and mashed
- 8 ounces cream cheese
- 1 small onion, chopped
- 2 eggs
- 2 to 3 tablespoons flour
- ½ to 1 cup parmesan cheese
- 2 to 3 tablespoons milk
- 1 package crispy fried onions (if desired)

Preheat oven to 375 degrees. Peel and cut potatoes into cubes and boil until tender. Drain and mash potatoes. Chop onion into fine pieces. Place all ingredients into a bowl and mix with an electric mixer until light and fluffy. Pour mixture into a greased baking dish and sprinkle a generous layer of parmesan cheese over mixture. Cover dish with a lid or aluminum foil. Bake at 375 degrees for 30 minutes. Remove cover for last 10 minutes to crisp up parmesan cheese. Sprinkle with crispy fried onions just prior to serving.

This is my Grandma Joan's recipe and is a staple at any holiday dinner. Everyone raves about these potatoes and are always coming back for seconds (and thirds).

All types of potatoes work for this recipe except for red potatoes. They still taste great but always seem to come out soupy.

BUTTERNUT SQUASH PARMESAN

Submitted by: Debbie Wesselius

Prep time	Cook time	Serves
20 min	**40 min**	**6-8**

ingredients

- 1 butternut squash (2 lb) peeled, seeded and cut into 1-inch chunks
- 4 teaspoons olive oil, divided
- 1 onion, cut into 1 inch chunks
- ¼ teaspoon pepper
- ½ cup 25%-less-sodium chicken broth
- ¼ cup plus 1 tablespoon Kraft® 100% parmesan light grated cheese, divided

instructions

Heat oven to 425 degrees. Toss squash with 2 teaspoons oil, then spread to form even layer on rimmed baking sheet. Bake 20 minutes. Next, add onions, pepper and remaining oil; toss to coat. Spread to form an even layer and bake another 20 minutes or until vegetables are tender. Drizzle with broth, mix lightly. Sprinkle with ¼ cup cheese, toss to coat. Transfer to bowl and sprinkle with remaining cheese.

notes

A nice side dish to compliment any meal.

OLD FASHION
SCALLOPED POTATOES

Submitted by: Robyn Barstad

Prep time	Cook time	Serves
20 min	**1 hour**	**4**

- 4 to 5 potatoes, sliced thin
- 2 to 3 tablespoons flour
- 1 medium onion, grated
- 2 to 3 tablespoons butter
- 2 cups milk (approximately)
- 1 to 3 teaspoons salt (to taste)
- pepper to taste

Preheat oven to 350 degrees. Place half of the sliced potatoes in bottom of well greased baking dish. Sprinkle half of the salt, pepper, flour, onion and bits of butter. Layer remaining potatoes, top with remaining salt, pepper, flour, onion, and butter. Add sufficient milk, so it can be seen between the top slices. Cover and bake in oven at 350 degrees for 30 minutes, remove cover and continue baking for another 30 minutes or until potatoes are tender and brown.

This was my grandmother Essie's recipe, she had a wood stove and her food always tasted so good, something about an old wood stove. I have added bacon bits, or ham and cheese to this recipe, between layers. Enjoy Hearties!

ingredients

instructions

notes

BEET
POTATO SALAD

Submitted by: René Wallach

Prep time	Cook time	Serves
20 min	4 hours 15 min	12

ingredients

- 3 pounds (about 6 small) russet potatoes, peeled and cut into 1-inch pieces
- 1 can (15 oz) whole beets in juice, drained and cut into ¾-inch pieces (or 3 fresh beets roasted)
- 3 hard-boiled eggs, cut into quarters
- 1 medium onion, chopped
- 2 celery stalks, chopped
- ⅔ cup mayonnaise
- ⅔ cup evaporated milk
- 1 tablespoon yellow mustard
- 1 tablespoon white vinegar
- 2 teaspoons salt
- 1 teaspoon freshly ground black pepper
- Chopped fresh parsley (optional)

instructions

In large saucepan, add potatoes and cover with water; bring to a boil. Cook over medium-high heat until potatoes are tender; drain.

In a large bowl, add potatoes, beets and eggs. In a separate medium bowl, combine onion, celery, mayonnaise, evaporated milk, mustard, vinegar, salt and pepper. Gently fold dressing mixture into potato mixture. Store covered in refrigerator for at least 4 hours or overnight; stir occasionally.

notes

This is a fun alternative to traditional potato salad, especially if you love beets. It also turns to a pretty pink color that looks great on a table!

VEGETABLE CASSEROLE

Submitted by: Jodie Pattengale

Prep time	Cook time	Serves
30 min	**40 min**	**12**

- ½ cup mayonnaise
- 1 medium onion, finely chopped
- 1 (10 oz) can cream of mushroom soup
- 1 cup sharp cheddar cheese, shredded
- 1 (6 oz) seasoned croutons, crushed
- 2 cups cauliflower florets
- ½ cup butter, melted
- 2 cups broccoli
- 2 eggs

Preheat oven to 350 degrees. Cook vegetables separately in boiling water for 5 minutes and drain. Distribute evenly in greased 11 x 7 inch dish. Beat eggs and combine with mayonnaise, onion, mushroom soup, and ½ cup cheese. Pour evenly over vegetables. Sprinkle remaining cheese over top and level with back of spoon. Pour melted butter over entire contents. Sprinkle crushed croutons over melted butter. Bake for 40 minutes before serving.

For extra flavour, prepare ahead. The dish will blend and the croutons will absorb the melted butter. This has been a Thanksgiving and Christmas staple in our family for many years and is always the most requested dish!

NANA'S CORN PUDDING

Submitted by: Jennifer Poole

Prep time	Cook time	Serves
10 min	**45 min**	**6-8**

ingredients

- 2 eggs beaten
- ½ cup sugar
- ⅓ cup flour
- 1 can cream of corn
- 2 cans corn, drained
- 1 cup milk
- ¼ cup butter, cut in pats (slices)

instructions

Preheat oven to 350 degrees. Beat eggs, add sugar and flour. Add cream of corn and two cans drained corn. Add milk, stir and pour into greased 9 inch square baking dish. Place pats of butter strategically on top. Cook for 20 minutes, stir pudding to remove "set part" from the sides; stir to center. Continue cooking another 25 minutes. Pudding is finished when golden brown and set in the center.

notes

This is a family favorite from my Grandmother's kitchen. It still remains one of the most requested dishes when our family gets together. I actually double the recipe and use a 9 x 13 casserole dish because it goes so fast. When my husband joined our family for the first time at Thanksgiving before we were married, my brothers tried to convince him it tasted terrible so they would have more. They were teenagers at the time, but they still tell guests when we are all together not to bother trying the corn pudding.

MAC & CHEESE CASSEROLE

Submitted by: Eliza Wittig

Prep time	Cook time	Serves
10 min	**90 min**	**12**

- 2 cans creamed corn
- 2 cans regular corn (not drained)
- ½ cup butter, melted (or margarine)
- 3 cups macaroni
- 2 cups Cheez Whiz®

Preheat oven to 350 degrees.

Mix all ingredients. Pour in 9 x 13 greased pan.

Bake covered for an hour and a half or until macaroni is soft and it has thickened.

Can be made the night before and refrigerated.

SPANISH TORTILLA

Submitted by: Jacinta Beccar Varela

Prep time	Cook time	Serves
15 min	**30 min**	**8**

- 2 medium potatoes
- ½ onion
- 3 eggs
- 1 tablespoon garlic powder
- 1 teaspoon salt
- 1 teaspoon pepper
- Canola oil for cooking

Peel potatoes and cut into slices (like french fries). Heat oil in a frying pan and fry potatoes until golden. Remove potatoes from oil and place on plate or bowl with paper towel to dry the oil excess. Cube onion and cook in a pan with a tablespoon of oil until translucent. In a bowl, beat eggs, garlic, salt and pepper. Stir in onion and french fries. Place mixture in an 8-inch frying pan with 1 tablespoon of oil. Let the bottom cook for about 2 to 4 minutes until golden brown (the top shouldn't be cooked). Check the bottom with a spatula. Remove pan from the stove. (Here comes the tricky part). Place a plate (it should cover the whole pan) above it and as quickly as possible turn it over. Then transfer the tortilla back into pan on the stove and let the other side cook until golden brown. Enjoy!

Tortillas can be eaten warm or cold, as a main dish, as a side dish, as an appetizer, in a picnic, they are that wonderful!

CUCUMBER SALAD

Submitted by: Murlann Vaine

Prep time	Cook time	Serves
10 min	**none**	**4**

- 1 large cucumber
- 1 large sweet onion
- 1 pint heavy whipping cream
- 2 tablespoons white vinegar
- salt and pepper to taste

Peel large cucumber and slice, then put into bowl.

Peel onion and slice, add to cucumbers. Pour whipping cream over cucumbers and onions, add two tablespoons vinegar to cucumbers and whip with fork, salt and pepper to taste.

Put in fridge for one hour before serving.

SUMMER CORN SALAD

Submitted by: Lynda Foote

Prep time	Cook time	Serves
45 min	**none**	**12**

ingredients

- 3 cans corn, drained (or 4 cups cooked corn cut from the cob)
- 1 cup green pepper, diced
- 1 cup red pepper, diced
- 1 cup grape tomatoes halved or quartered
- ½ cup onion, finely diced (more if you like)
- 2 cups sharp cheddar cheese, grated
- 1 cup mayonnaise
- 1 bag Chili Cheese Fritos®, crushed

instructions

Clean and dice green peppers, red peppers, grape tomatoes and onion.

Mix peppers and onions with drained corn, then add tomatoes. Stir in cheese and mayonnaise, then chill.

Mix in crushed Fritos® just before serving.

notes

This salad does not last long around our house. It's a great side for summer barbecues and pot lucks.

CHOCOLATE GRAVY

Submitted by: Haley Brown

Prep time	Cook time	Serves
5 min	**15 min**	**5-6**

ingredients

- 1 cup sugar
- ½ cup flour
- ¼ cup cocoa powder
- 1 cup hot water
- 1 cup milk
- 1 tablespoon vanilla
- 1 tablespoon butter

instructions

In a mixing bowl, mix together your sugar, flour and cocoa powder. Mix with a whisk to get most of the lumps out. Stir in hot water until mixed well, then stir in milk. Add mixture to a sauce pan over medium heat and cook until it becomes desired thickness for a gravy, stir constantly (I like to use a whisk to stir it during the cooking process). Once it is at desired thickness, remove from heat and add vanilla and butter. Mix well and serve over warm biscuits.

notes

This is truly a go to "comfort food" from my childhood. It's easy to make and tastes so good over a warm buttered biscuit.

Can't you just imagine the children of Hope Valley families being so excited for Abigail to serve this at her cafe???

I hope you enjoy this recipe as much as I do!

CREAMY GRAPE SALAD

Submitted by: Eliza Wittig

Prep time	Cook time	Serves
20 min	**none**	**15**

ingredients

- 4 pounds grapes
- 8 ounces cream cheese
- 8 ounces sour cream
- ½ cup sugar
- 1 cup brown sugar
- 1 cup walnuts

instructions

Wash grapes and dry completely. In a medium bowl, mix cream cheese, sour cream, and sugar to make a dressing. Add grapes to dressing, stir. In a seperate bowl, mix brown sugar and nuts, sprinkle over top of grape mixture.

BASIL
PASTA SALAD

Submitted by: Olivia Anderson

Prep time	Cook time	Serves
20 min	**10 min**	**4-6**

- 1 package of any pasta (macaroni or shells recommended)
- ½ large cucumber
- ⅛ teaspoon pepper
- ⅛ teaspoon salt
- 6 teaspoons basil pesto
- 1 red bell pepper
- 1 teaspoon olive oil

Start by boiling pasta according to time written on package, usually around 8 to 10 minutes.

Chop pepper into small pieces. Slice cucumber and then cut slices into quarters. When pasta is finished boiling, drain and run under cold water, mixing it thoroughly until pasta is cold; strain.

Add cucumbers and peppers and mix them into pasta. Stir in salt, pepper, and pesto. Refrigerate for 5 minutes (optional).

RENEE'S MACARONI SALAD

Submitted by: Lori Meeker

Prep time 30-40 min	Cook time 10 min	Serves 8-10

ingredients

- 6 hard boiled eggs, diced
- 6 cups cooked pasta (rotini, penne or whatever you like)
- ¼ cup onion, chopped
- 2 stalks celery, diced
- 1 ½ cups Miracle Whip® or mayonnaise
- 1 ½ tablespoons yellow mustard
- 2 tablespoons cider vinegar
- ½ cup sugar
- ¼ cup milk
- 1 teaspoon salt (optional)

instructions

In a mixing bowl, mix Miracle Whip® (mayonnaise) with mustard, vinegar, sugar, milk, and salt (optional). Add pasta, onion, celery and egg.

Stir to blend. Chill before serving.

notes

Dedicated to my sister-in-law, Renee Thomas, who shared this recipe with me many, many years ago. This is a family favorite!

The time listed includes boiling the pasta. Hard boiling the eggs may take a bit longer.

PASTA SALAD

Submitted by: Beka T

Prep time	Cook time	Serves
30 min	**15 min**	**12**

- 1 (1 lb) box tricolor pasta twists
- ½ pound provolone cheese
  (from deli ⅛ in sliced)
- ¼ pound hard salami
  (from deli ⅛ in sliced)
- ½ pound pepperoni
  (from deli ⅛ in sliced)
- 3 to 4 medium tomatoes, chopped
- 2 stalks celery, chopped
- 2 green peppers, diced
- 1 onion, diced

Dressing:
- ¾ cup olive oil
- ¼ cup vinegar
- 1 tablespoon oregano
- salt and pepper to taste

Cook pasta per instructions on box. Chop provolone cheese, hard salami and pepperoni into small squares. Dice green peppers, onion, celery and tomatoes. Combine cheese, salami, pepperoni, onion, celery, green peppers and tomatoes into large bowl. Once pasta is done, add to the rest of ingredients. For the dressing, add olive oil, vinegar, oregano and a pinch of salt and pepper to a bowl with lid and shake to combine. Once combined, add to salad stir and refrigerate. Ta Da! You're done!

It's best served cold and will last up to 5 days in the refrigerator.

SPAGHETTI SALAD

Submitted by: Sharon Stark

Prep time	Cook time	Serves
15 min	10 min	10-12

- 1 (1 lb) box thin spaghetti
- 3 to 4 scallions, chopped
- 1 medium to large green pepper, chopped
- 1 (8 to 16 oz) bottle Zesty Italian dressing
- 1 bottle McCormick® Salad Supreme seasoning

Cook spaghetti according to directions on package. Rinse and drain under cold water. Put a portion of spaghetti into serving bowl. Add some green peppers, scallions and Salad Supreme, mix very well. Repeat until all ingredients have been used and tossed thoroughly. Put in refrigerator to chill well before serving.

Easy recipe to do for immediate use. Can be put in freezer if you need to chill in a hurry or done overnight and chilled in the fridge for a future event.

This recipe was given to my mother by a friend years ago and she passed it on to me. It has become one of my most requested recipes.

BROCCOLI TOMATO SALAD

Submitted by: Karla Griffin

Prep time	Cook time	Serves
15-20 min	**6-8 hours**	**6-8**

- 1 medium head of broccoli, washed and separated into florets
- 1 ½ cups cherry tomatoes, washed and cut into halves
- 1 (4.25 oz) can sliced black olives
- 1 (8 oz) can sliced water chestnuts
- 3 to 4 green onions, sliced
- 1 (16 oz) bottle Italian dressing
- ½ cup fresh mushrooms, sliced (may substitute 1 (4.5 oz) jar of sliced mushrooms)

Drain and wash all canned vegetables and pat dry. Mix all vegetables together in a large bowl. Pour 1 ½ cups Italian dressing over all vegetables. Let salad marinate for 6 to 8 hours in refrigerator prior to serving. Stir salad at least once while marinating.

Our family makes this tasty salad each Christmas due to its beautifully mixed vegetables.

TACO SALAD

Submitted by: Debbie Wesselius

Prep time	Cook time	Serves
20 min	**10 min**	**6**

ingredients

- 1 pound hamburger
- 1 packet taco seasoning
- 1 head of lettuce
- 1 onion, chopped fine
- 2 tomatoes, chopped fine
- 1 cup cheese, shredded
- 1 cup mayonnaise
- ⅓ cup sugar
- 1 large bag zesty cheese or nacho tortilla chips, coarsely crushed

instructions

Cook hamburger with half of the taco seasoning. Then add lettuce, onion, tomatoes and cheese to hamburger; toss. In a separate bowl, combine mayonnaise, sugar and remaining taco seasoning. Combine the two mixtures.

Crush tortilla chips and mix together. Best to add chips just prior to serving. Serves six.

notes

You can also add your favourite can of beans and sliced olives to this recipe.

CASHEW SALAD

Submitted by: Judy Milder

Prep time	Cook time	Serves
15 min	**none**	**6-8**

- Romaine lettuce, torn into bite size pieces
- 1 cup Swiss cheese, cut up
- 1 cup cashews
- bacon bits

Dressing:
- 1 cup salad oil
- ⅔ cup sugar or equivalent of sugar substitute
- ⅓ cup salad vinegar
- dash of mineral salt
- ¼ teaspoon dry mustard
- 1 teaspoon poppy seeds

Layer salad ingredients in a salad bowl. Combine dressing ingredients and mix well. Pour desired amount over salad just before serving.

Toss and serve. Enjoy!

OUR FAMILY'S BROCCOLI SALAD

Submitted by: Lynda Foote

Prep time	Cook time	Serves
20 min	**none**	**6-8**

- 2 to 3 heads of broccoli, cut into bite sized pieces
- 1 pound cooked crispy bacon pieces
- ½ cup dried cranberries or raisins
- 2 to 3 green onions, sliced thin
- ¼ cup sunflower seeds

Dressing:
- 1 cup mayonnaise
- ¼ cup (or less) white sugar
- 2 to 3 tablespoons vinegar

Cut and slice broccoli and green onions; toss together. Add cranberries (or raisins) and sunflower seeds. Mix dressing ingredients until smooth. Pour over veggies and toss until covered; chill. Just prior to serving, add bacon pieces.

I found this basic recipe in a school fundraiser cookbook years ago. It's been adjusted and added to as years have passed. It's the dish I am asked to bring for extended family gatherings.

I usually have to triple it so we have leftovers to enjoy at home. Thank goodness our big box store carries huge bags of fresh broccoli pieces when those times come!

STRAWBERRY ROMAINE SALAD

Submitted by: Traci LaRosa

Prep time	Cook time	Serves
15-20 min	**none**	**6-8**

ingredients

- 1 head romaine lettuce, torn into bite-size pieces
- 1 pint strawberries, sliced
- 1 red onion, diced
- ¼ cup sunflower seeds

Dressing:
- 1 cup mayonaise
- ¼ cup vinegar
- ⅔ cup sugar
- 2 tablespoons poppy seeds

instructions

In a large bowl, mix together lettuce, strawberries, red onion and sunflower seeds. Set aside. For dressing, in a small bowl mix mayonaise, vinegar, sugar and poppy seeds. Just before serving, pour over the salad mixture and gently toss, reserving any leftover dressing in the refrigerator.

notes

As a military spouse of 21 years, I've collected recipes from each of the nine places we've lived. This recipe was given to me in Hawaii and I love that it's just a fresh, easy salad to whip up!

SPINACH RAINBOW SALAD

Submitted by: Kami Clements

Prep time	Cook time	Serves
20 min	5 min	8

- ½ cup strawberries, sliced
- 4 to 5 cups spinach
- ½ cup blueberries
- ¼ cup sugar
- ⅓ cup Swiss cheese, shredded
- ½ to ⅔ cup pecans
- ⅓ cup mandarin oranges, drained

Dressing:

- ¾ cup olive oil
- ⅓ cup sugar
- ⅓ cup red wine vinegar
- 1 teaspoon poppy seeds
- ½ teaspoon onion, minced
- ¾ teaspoon salt
- ½ teaspoon Dijon mustard

Put sugar and pecans in a skillet over medium-high heat and heat until well-coated and slightly caramelized. In a large bowl, toss pecans and other salad ingredients. Mix dressing ingredients well and pour on tossed salad. For best results serve immediately.

Leftover dressing can be stored in an airtight container in the fridge for up to 2 weeks.

Family favorite for years!

CHICKEN/RICE SALAD

Submitted by: Wendy Vandermay

Prep time	Cook time	Serves
30 min	**Chill for several hours**	**6**

- 2 cups cooked chicken, diced
- 1 tablespoon salad oil
- 1 tablespoon orange juice
- ½ teaspoon salt
- 1 ½ cups cooked white rice
- 1 cup seedless green grapes
- 1 cup celery, chopped
- 1 can pineapple tidbits
- 1 can mandarin oranges, drained
- ½ cup slivered almonds
- 1 cup mayonnaise

Mix all ingredients together.

Chill for several hours or overnight. Serve and Enjoy!

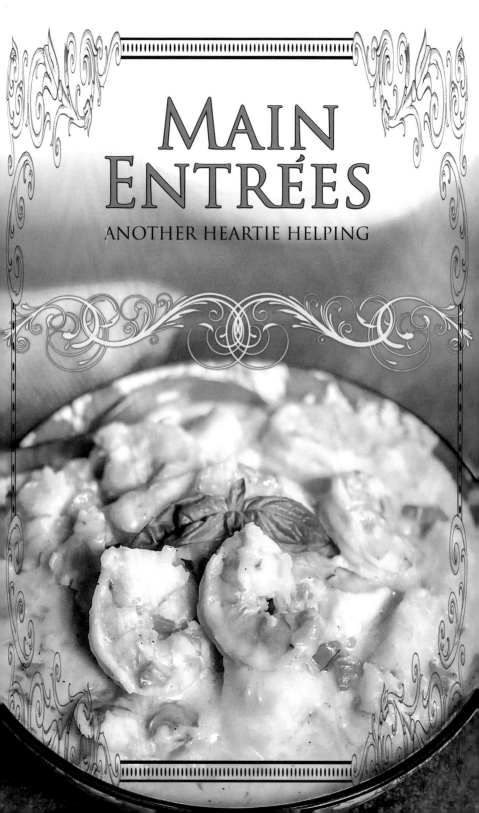

Main Entrées

Another Heartie Helping

RUSSIAN CHICKEN

Submitted by: Luanne Maroney

Prep time 15-20 min	Cook time 90 min	Serves 4-6

- 2 pounds chicken pieces or 4 to 6 chicken breasts (bone in or boneless fillets)
- 1 (16 oz) jar apricot preserves
- 2 packages dry onion soup mix
- 1 bottle Russian salad dressing
- vegetable oil

Preheat oven to 325 degrees. Sear chicken pieces in a skillet, with a little vegetable oil on each side, until about half cooked. Then place chicken in a large 13 x 9 glass dish that has been coated with cooking spray. Add apricot preserves on top of chicken pieces. Mix packages of dry onion soup mix and Russian dressing together in a small bowl. Pour mixture over chicken. Bake approximately 1 ½ hours. You can add a little water to dressing mixture if it is too thick. Check pieces with a fork after 60 minutes. Depending on your oven, cooking time can vary.

The only reason this is called "Russian Chicken" is because of the use of the dressing. At least, this is what my family has always called it. It comes out very tasty with a bit of a sweet taste from the preserves. I like serving it with rice or scalloped potatoes as a side with a salad or green vegetable. It's a nice dish for company and really doesn't take much prep and few ingredients. Once in oven, I can work on other side dishes, etc.

HONEY GLAZED CHICKEN

Submitted by: Jina Shawback

Prep time	Cook time	Serves
20 min	1 hour and 20 min	4

- ½ cup all-purpose flour
- ½ teaspoon cayenne pepper
- 1 fryer chicken, cut up (3 lb)
- ½ cup butter, melted (divide)
- ¼ cup brown sugar, packed
- ¼ cup honey
- ¼ cup lemon juice
- 1 tablespoon soy sauce
- 1 ½ teaspoon curry powder
- 1 teaspoon salt

Preheat oven to 350 degrees. In a bag, combine flour, salt, and cayenne pepper. Then add chicken pieces and shake to coat. Pour 4 tablespoons butter into a 9 x 13 x 2 baking pan, place chicken in pan, turning pieces once to coat.

Bake uncovered at 350 degrees for 30 minutes. Combine brown sugar, honey, lemon juice, soy sauce, curry powder, and remaining butter. Pour over chicken.

Bake 45 minutes more or until chicken is tender, basting several times with pan drippings.

BBQ PORK RIND COATED
BAKED CHICKEN BREAST

Submitted by: Jennilyn Helms

Prep time	Cook time	Serves
10 min	45-60 min	4

- 4 medium-large boneless skinless chicken breast
- 1 bag BBQ flavored pork rinds
- ¼ teaspoon pepper
- 3 eggs

Preheat oven to 350 degrees. In a large bowl, crush pork rinds until there are no big chunks left. Add pepper to pork rinds and mix.

In a second large bowl, break 3 eggs and stir. Fully dip each chicken breast in egg then in pork rinds and coat thoroughly. Place on a baking sheet or tin pan.

Cook uncovered at 350 degrees for 45 to 60 minutes (stoves vary so the time may as well).

Keto-Friendly!

ingredients

instructions

notes

OVEN FRIED PARMESAN CHICKEN

Submitted by: Lindsey Stephens

Prep time	Cook time	Serves
10 min	**20-25 min**	**4**

ingredients

- 1 ½ pounds chicken breast tenders (one package)
- 1 egg
- 1 cup plain bread crumbs
- ¼ cup parmesan cheese
- 1 to 2 tablespoons seasoning salt (or to taste)

instructions

Preheat the oven to 400 degrees. Crack egg into a glass bowl and beat lightly.

In a large zip top bag, mix together the bread crumbs, parmesan cheese, and seasoning salt to taste.

Dip chicken in egg and place into bag. Fill bag half way full of egg coated chicken. Seal bag and shake to cover chicken.

Place chicken on a greased cookie sheet. Repeat with remaining chicken.

Bake for about 20 minutes until done.

MOM'S BUFFALO WING MARINADE

Submitted by: Helen Pearson

Prep time 10 min	Cook time 45 min	Serves 4

- ½ cup apple cider vinegar
- ¼ cup soy sauce
- ½ cup ketchup
- ¼ cup honey
- ½ cup brown sugar
- 2 tablespoons yellow mustard
- 2 pounds chicken wings
- 2 tablespoons lemon juice
- 2 tablespoons Dale's® seasoning
- 1 clove garlic, minced (or use a garlic press)
- 1 teaspoon paprika
- 1 teaspoon ground ginger

Mix all ingredients well. Pour over 2 pounds of chicken wings (cut into drumsticks and flats with tips removed). Cover and marinate for 6 to 8 hours or overnight. To bake, place a cooling rack on rimmed cookie sheet. Put chicken wings on rack evenly spaced and bake at 400 degrees for 45 to 50 minutes until crispy. To grill, place chicken on grill over moderate heat until browned and crispy. To smoke chicken, follow your smoker's directions and use your favorite wood (we use pecan or oak) to smoke the wings. We've smoked them at 225 to 250 degrees for 2 to 2 ½ hours. Discard the remaining marinade.

Mom loved making this for family cookouts. She perfected the recipe over several years and once she got it right, as she said, she asked me to type the recipe for her. Mom was a caterer and loved cooking for family and friends until she passed away in December 2015. I still use her recipe to make wings. And Mom was a "Heartie". She called Jack, "My Mountie!" -Lori Pearson

HOT HAM SANDWICHES

Submitted by: Nancy Butler

Prep time	Cook time	Serves
30 min	30 min	6-8

ingredients

- ½ cup butter
- 2 tablespoons onion, minced
- 1 tablespoon poppy seed
- 2 tablespoons yellow prepared mustard
- 1 pound shaved ham
- 8 slices Kraft® processed Swiss cheese

instructions

Preheat oven to 350 degrees. Mix first 4 ingredients and spread on both sides of buns. Divide ham onto buns and add 1 slice cheese to each sandwich.

Wrap in heavy duty foil and bake at 350 degrees for 30 minutes.

Enjoy hot out of the oven!

notes

My mother would make big batches of these ham sandwiches when we all gathered together.

They are so tasty and go great with potato salad.

CHICKEN ROLL-UPS

Submitted by: Jina Shawback

Prep time	Cook time	Serves
20 min	**30-40 min**	**8**

- 2 cups chicken, cooked and chopped
- 8 ounces cream cheese
- ½ cup cheddar cheese, grated
- 2 tablespoons mild salsa
- ¼ cup chopped onions
- 1 teaspoon salt
- 2 cans crescent rolls

Preheat oven to 375 degrees. In a medium bowl, mix first 6 ingredients together. Lay out cresent roll dough. Place some of the mixture on flattened crescent roll and roll up. Continue until all rolls are used. Then place in baking pan.

Bake at 375 degrees until rolls are golden brown. Then serve!

CHICKEN VEGGIE CASSEROLE

Submitted by: Myra Trent

Prep time	Cook time	Serves
30 min	**1 hour**	**4-6**

ingredients

- 4 chicken pieces, diced
- 1 onion, diced
- 5 potatoes, diced
- 2 carrots, diced
- 1 can cream of chicken soup
- 1 cup of water
- 1 (8 oz) container sour cream
- pepper to taste
- ¼ teaspoon salt
- ½ teaspoon sage
- ½ teaspoon thyme
- ½ teaspoon rosemary
- ½ teaspoon poultry seasoning
- 1 tablespoon parsley flakes
- 2 packages Ritz® crackers, crushed
- ½ cup butter (or margarine), melted

instructions

Preheat oven to 350 degrees. Cut up chicken into small chunks and cook in cup of water, boil until done.

In a glass 13 x 9 dish, mix onion, potatoes and carrots. Sprinkle with spices and mix in cooked chicken chunks, mix well. Pour water, cream of chicken soup and sour cream over mixture and mix well.

Spread crushed Ritz® crackers over chicken mixture and sprinkle with melted butter.

Place dish in oven for 1 hour. Serve with ranch or blue cheese dressing.

CHICKEN SPAGHETTI

Submitted by: Angie Duerden

Prep time 45 - 50 min	Cook time 45 min	Serves 10-12

- 2 cups cooked shredded chicken
- 3 cups dry spaghetti, broken into 2 inch pieces
- 2 cans cream of chicken soup
- 2 cups cheese, grated
- 1 small onion, diced
- 1 cup mushrooms, sliced
- 2 cups chicken broth
- red pepper flakes

Preheat oven to 350 degrees. Spray 9x13 inch pan with non-stick spray. Shred chicken and set aside. Sauté diced onion with mushrooms. Cook spaghetti in 2 cups of chicken broth, add water if needed. Do not overcook. In a large bowl, add drained spaghetti, soup, onions, mushrooms, 1 cup shredded cheese, a little bit of red pepper flakes if you like them and chicken with a bit of chicken broth to thin mixture out.

Put in prepared pan add the rest of the cheese on top. Bake for 45 minutes, you can add some foil the last 10 minutes (make sure it doesn't cover it all the way, don't want the cheese to stick to the foil).

A family recipe that is one of those comfort foods. It is delicious!

TOURTIERE
(PORK PIE)

Submitted by: Sharon Peltier Stark

Prep time 30-40min	Cook time 30 min	Serves 6-8

ingredients

- 1 pound lean ground pork
- 1 cup water
- ⅛ teaspoon ground sage
- ½ cup onion, finely chopped
- ½ cup dry bread crumbs
- ½ to 1 teaspoon poultry seasoning
- dash of ground nutmeg
- dash of pepper
- 1 teaspoon salt
- pastry for 2 (9 inch) pie crusts

instructions

Preheat oven to 400 degrees. Brown ground pork in skillet then drain off excess fat. Stir in water, onion, bread crumbs, salt, sage, pepper, nutmeg, and poultry seasoning. Simmer uncovered untill onion is tender, about 20 minutes, stirring often. Line pie plate with pastry, fill with meat mixture. Adjust top crust, seal and flute edges. Cut slits in top of crust.

Bake at 400 degrees until golden brown, about 30 minutes. Cover edge of pastry with foil, if necessary to prevent over browning.

notes

This recipe was passed down from my great grandmother who was from Quebec, Canada - it is a tradition for my family to have this for dinner on New Year's Day.

CROCK-POT® CHICKEN SWEET POTATOES

Submitted by: Sarah Storm

Prep time	Cook time	Serves
10-15 min	5-6 hours	4-6

- 4 to 6 boneless chicken breasts (or 2 to 3 pounds)
- 1 ½ cups chicken broth (organic)
- 2 tablespoon Italian seasoning
- 1 tablespoon garlic powder
- 1 tablespoon onion powder
- 1 teaspoon oregano
- 1 teaspoon basil
- 2 to 3 sweet potatoes, cut into cubes

Mix all seasoning into a bowl. Turn Crock-Pot® on low and put chicken into the Crock-Pot®. Cut up sweet potatoes and make sure to cover chicken with sweet potatoes.

With combined seasonings, add chicken broth, mix together and pour into Crock-Pot®.

Keep Crock-Pot® on low heat for 5 to 6 hours until chicken is cooked and sweet potatoes are soft.

Serve on a plate for a warm fall or winter meal!

This recipe is perfect for those with dairy, gluten or sugar sensitivites.

PORK CHOP & POTATO BAKE

Submitted by: Marti Neidigh

Prep time	Cook time	Serves
30 min	**1 hour 15 min**	**6**

ingredients

- 6 boneless pork chops
- 10 to 12 potatoes, peeled and sliced
- 1 (16 oz) cheddar cheese, shredded
- 1 cup chicken broth
- ½ cup butter
- ¼ cup milk
- onion powder
- parsley flakes
- salt and pepper to taste
- cooking spray

instructions

Preheat oven to 350 degrees. Spray frying pan with cooking spray and put on medium-high heat. Season chops on both sides with salt, pepper and onion powder. Brown chops well on both sides, remove from pan. Add chicken broth to pan to de-glaze. Place layer of sliced potatoes in casserole dish, add salt, pepper and onion powder to taste. Dot with butter and sprinkle parsley flakes over potatoes. Add chops over layered potatoes, then repeat until all potatoes have been added. Next pour de-glazed liquid over casserole, cover with aluminum foil and bake for 1 hour. When casserole is almost done baking, make the cheese sauce. Melt cheese and ¼ cup milk until well incorporated. When potatoes and chops are tender (after 1 hour) pour cheese sauce over entire casserole and place back into oven uncovered. Let bake until brown on top (15 minutes or until desired color).

notes

This recipe was a favorite of my family growing up. Note: You can also use chicken in place of pork chops.

HALUSHKY

Submitted by: Kathy Garchar

Prep time	Cook time	Serves
15 min	**1 hour**	**8**

- 2 cups butter (1 lb)
- 2 (8 oz) packages kolbasi or smoked sausage, sliced
- 4 medium onions, chopped
- 1 large head of cabbage
- 2 (1 lb) packages wide hearth style noodles
- 8 medium white potatoes, peeled and cubed
- salt and pepper to taste

Boil cubed potatoes for 15 minutes. Drain and set aside. Remove outer leaves of cabbage, cut into 4 pieces around the core. Throw out core. Chop cabbage into medium pieces and boil ½ hour on high heat. Drain and set aside. Boil noodles for 10 minutes, adding a pinch of salt and a little vegetable oil to water. Drain and set aside. In large frying pan, melt 1 cup butter, sauté onions on medium heat about 5 minutes, stirring often. Add kolbasi or smoked sausage to onions and cook another 10 minutes, stirring often. Add remaining butter and let melt, stir. Turn heat to low. In a large serving dish, put the cabbage, potatoes, and noodles. Pour over the onions, meat and butter mixture and gently mix all together. Salt and pepper to taste. Enjoy!

This is my mom's (Helen) recipe for Polish style Halushky (ha-loosh-key). She learned to make this from her mom, my grandmother, from Poland, Mary Gavalinski. It is a hearty meal and great comfort food. You can prepare the potatoes and cabbage a day before and refrigerate if you like. Then just heat them up in the microwave before adding to the mixture. I have named this recipe that I love so much for the town I love so much Hope Valley Halushki.

HONEY SOY GINGER STIR FRY

Submitted by: Kristyn Press

Prep time	Cook time	Serves
45 min	**15 min**	**6**

- ½ cup soy sauce
- ¾ cup brown sugar
- 4 tablespoons honey
- 5 centimeter piece ginger
- 2 teaspoons sesame oil
- 2 small brown onions, thinly sliced
- 2 cloves garlic, diced
- ¼ cup peanut oil
- 1 tablespoon corn flour (or thickening agent)
- 1 cup water
- 1 pound pork fillet or chicken breast
- 2 cups basmati rice (to serve)
- choice of mixed vegetables (to serve)

Combine soy sauce and brown sugar in a saucepan and bring to a boil. Mix soy and sugar mixture with honey, ginger and sesame oil in a bowl. Add choice of meat. Stir to coat, cover and refrigerate for 20 to 30 minutes to marinate. Heat wok over high heat, add 1 tablespoon peanut oil.

Drain and reserve marinade from meat. Add half of the meat to wok and stir fry for 2 minutes or until sealed. Transfer to a bowl. Repeat using 1 tablespoon oil and remaining meat. Then add remaining oil to wok, stir fry choice of vegetables and remaining marinade for 2 minutes.

Return meat to wok and add water and corn flour. Stir and cook for a further minute or until sauce is thickened. Serve with rice.

SEAFOOD CASSEROLE SUPREME

Submitted by: Debbie Wesselius

Prep time	Cook time	Serves
30 min	**30 min**	**6-8**

- 2 cups onion, chopped
- 2 cups celery, diced
- ½ cup plus 2 tablespoons butter
- ½ cup flour
- 4 cups milk
- 1 teaspoon salt
- ¼ teaspoon pepper

- ½ pound cheddar cheese
- 10 ounces lobster
- ½ pound crabmeat
- ½ pound shrimp
- ½ pound scallops
  ½ pound fillets (haddock)

Preheat oven to 325 degrees. Sauté onions and celery in 2 tablespoon butter until softened. Add salt, pepper and set aside. In a large pot, melt butter over low heat. Then blend in flour. Stir over low heat until smooth and bubbly. Next, stir in milk. Heat until boiling and milk starts to thicken. Add cheese and cook until cheese is melted. Add celery and onions. Then add seafood of your choice. Place in large casserole dish and bake at 325 degrees for 20 to 30 minutes. Take out when finished and enjoy!

This was handed down to me from my mother and is a family favorite. I often make it for special occasions.

MARYLAND CRAB BISQUE

Submitted by: Katherine Momcilovich

Prep time 20 min	Cook time 45 - 60 min	Serves 8-10

- 2 stalks celery, chopped
- 1 large onion, chopped
- ½ cup butter
- 1 quart half and half
- 1 quart heavy whipping cream
- 1 (32 oz) container seafood stock
- 1 (16 oz) can crab meat (purchase from the seafood section of grocery store)
- ¼ cup Old Bay® seasoning
- 1 to 2 tablespoons gluten free flour (thickener)

Start by melting butter in the bottom of a large stock pot. Add chopped celery and onion and allow it to simmer at just between medium and low. Cook for about 6 to 7 minutes slowly turning over the onions and celery.

Then add crab and seafood stock, as well as Old Bay® seasoning. ¼ cup of Old Bay® is good but I like mine spicier, so I may add a pinch or two or three more. Then add in half and half and heavy whipping cream. And the final touches of a tablespoon or 2 of gluten free flour to thicken it up.

Then turn up the heat between medium and medium high and stir every so often for another 45 minutes until it's done. It's great the first day and sometimes even better the second day.

VA'S KALE SOUP

Submitted by: Ann Avila

Prep time	Cook time	Serves
30 -45 min	**about 2 hours**	**6-8**

- 4 cups kale, chopped
- 4 pounds meaty soup bone (or 3 pounds chicken breast, chopped)
- 3 to 4 potatoes, peeled and chopped
- ½ head of cabbage, chopped
- 4 garlic cloves, minced
- 1 large onion, chopped
- 3 celery stalks, chopped
- salt and pepper to taste

Variations:
- Linguica sausage, sliced (Portuguese sausage, adds lots of flavor)
- small bag frozen mixed vegetables
- can white beans, rinsed
- egg noodles or white rice

Boil soup bone or chicken in a large soup pot until meat is done, about 1 hour. Remove soup bone, pull off meat. Add meat back in plus kale, potatoes, cabbage, garlic, onions, celery and seasonings, and any variations to the broth. Simmer for one hour or so. Serve with fresh sliced French bread. NOTE: This soup freezes well!

My brother and I grew up down the street from my Va (Grandma in Portuguese) who is no longer with us. We remember many Saturdays receiving a call from her inviting us to come down for lunch. We would always ask her if we were having green soup. That's what we called it growing up! Many years later, I asked her for the recipe and all she could tell me was a list of things that she would put in it...there were no measured amounts of ingredients and there was no written recipe. She used what she had on hand and the kale

was grown in the backyard. I wrote everything down on a small piece of paper which is still in my recipe card file. Very seldom was it exactly the same, but it was always wonderful! This recipe is full proof...you can't mess it up! I've had it published in other cookbooks and have given out the recipe many times. Today, friends and family are quick to accept an invite when they know I'm making a pot of this soup. Enjoy!!!

TEAR SOUP
(OLD FASHIONED VEGGIE SOUP)

Submitted by: Lucy Luginbill

Prep time	Cook time	Serves
20-30 min	45 min to 1 hour	10-12

ingredients

- 1 pound hamburger
- 1 (16 oz) bag of peeled carrots, chopped
- 1 large onion, chopped
- 1-2 celery stalks, chopped
- 1 green pepper, chopped
- 1 yellow or red pepper, chopped
- ½ to 1 cup fresh parsley
- vegetables options: broccoli, canned corn, chopped green beans, etc.
- 1 clove garlic, minced
- 1 teaspoon chili powder
- ½ teaspoon thyme
- Bay leaf
- ½ to ⅓ of a 46 ounce V8® juice
- 2 (15 oz) cans diced tomatoes
- 1 or 2 cans water, use tomato cans
- Salt and pepper to taste
- ¼ cup barley or rice (optional)

instructions

In a large soup kettle, brown the hamburger and then add the fresh vegetables. Stir occasionally for about 5 minutes. Add remaining ingredients. Bring to boil and then simmer for 45 minutes or more. Serve with sourdough bread (bread bowls are nice, too) and a side salad.

notes

I call this soup "Tear Soup" because you can make it with a friend when they need comfort. Chopping the veggies and adding ingredients to the soup kettle provides an opportunity to listen, talk, and share tears. You may also want to bring the book, *Tear Soup* to read; a picture book about grief for all ages by Pat Schwiebert. It is very gentle and comforting for anyone who is experiencing loss of any kind.

CROCK-POT®
SPLIT PEA SOUP

Submitted by: Debbie Wesselius

Prep time 15 min	Cook time 4-5 hours (high) 8-10 hours (low)	Serves 8-10

- 1 pound dried green split peas, rinsed (or 2¼ cups) dry uncooked split peas = 5 cups cooked)
- 1 meaty ham bone, 2 ham hocks or 2 cups ham, diced
- 1 cup baby carrots, sliced
- 1 cup yellow onion, chopped
- 2 stalks celery plus leaves, chopped
- 2 cloves garlic, minced
- ¼ cup fresh parsley, chopped
- 6 cups chicken broth
- 2 to 3 smoked sausages, quartered and sliced
- salt and pepper to taste
- 1 bay leaf

Layer all ingredients in slow cooker except for the sausage. Do not stir ingredients. Cover and cook on high 4 to 5 hours or 8 to 10 hours on low until peas are very soft and ham falls off the bone. Add smoked sausages during the last hour of cooking. Serve when ready.

This is one of my husband's favorite recipes. Called Snert in the Netherlands where he was born. It is the easiest version of it that I have found to make.

CORN CHOWDER

Submitted by: Eliza Wittig

Prep time	Cook time	Serves
20 min	**under an hour**	**12**

ingredients

- 1 pound bacon, chopped
- 1 cup onion, chopped
- 2 cups water
- 8 medium potatoes, cubed
- 2 cans cream of chicken soup
- 2 cups sour cream (light is fine)
- 3 cups milk
- 2 cans corn (not drained)
- 2 teaspoons parsley
- salt and pepper to taste

instructions

Sauté bacon and onion in a large pot, then drain.

Add water, potatoes and corn. Simmer 15 to 20 minutes (until potatoes are soft).

Add soup and sour cream. Gradually add milk, then spices.

Heat to serving temperature but do not boil. Enjoy!

EASY FAMILY FAVORITE

Submitted by: Pam Evans

Prep time	Cook time	Serves
10 min	**15 min**	**6**

- 1 pound lean hamburger
- 1 packet taco seasoning
- 2 (15 oz) cans dark red kidney beans
- 2 (15 oz) cans tomato sauce
- 1 can small olives
- 1 bag Doritos® Nacho cheese*
- 1 ½ cup Mexican cheese, shredded (* This recipe is gluten free. If you use a different brand of chips it may not be gluten free)

Brown 1 to 1 ½ pounds hamburger in a large pan and then drain the fat. Add taco seasoning and water as directed on the package. Stir well and simmer for 5 minutes. Add kidney beans including liquid. Add tomato sauce. Drain olives and mix well. Take about 1 cup of chips and crumble with your hand until pieces are about 1 inch in size. Add to mixture and stir in well. Then add about 1 cup cheese and stir. Heat for 10 to 15 minutes over low heat, stirring a few times. When chips have broken down and mix has thickened, it is done. Sprinkle remaining cheese over the top and serve with remaining chips on the side. Tastes great reheated if you have leftovers which is rare.

I got a basic recipe from a coworker's wife in the 1980's. I have modified it over the years & made it my own (gluten-free). After cooking the meat, you can put all the ingredients in a Crock-Pot® on low & take to a pot luck, picnic, etc. When shared with others I usually double the recipe. It's also very attractive looking. This can be made without the beans if they are a dietary issue.

COWBOY SOUP

Submitted by: Cheryl Riley

Prep time	Cook time	Serves
10 min	**1 hour**	**6-8**

- 1 small onion chopped
- 1 ½ pounds ground beef
- 2 (15 oz) cans mixed vegetables
- 1 (15 oz) can Rotel® diced tomatoes and green chilies
- 2 (15 oz) cans stewed tomatoes
- 1 small can English peas
- 1 small can Shoepeg corn
- 1 box Spanish rice

Cook onions and beef together until done, then drain.

Add all ingredients (including juices from can) to a 2 quart or larger soup pot.

Simmer for 1 hour stirring occasionally. Serve with cornbread or crackers.

This was my grandmother's recipe and it is very popular. I take it to church potlucks or just enjoy with family or friends. It's easy to prepare and very delicious.

5-INGREDIENT WHITE CHICKEN CHILI

Submitted by: Beth Burdick

Prep time	Cook time	Serves
5 min	**1hr or 8hrs**	**6-8**

- 1 to 1 ½ cups favorite jarred salsa (depending on how spicy you like it!)
- 2 ½ to 3 pounds frozen chicken breasts or tenderloins
- 4 (15 oz) cans northern white beans, drained and rinsed
- 4 cups chicken broth
- 1 tablespoon dried oregano

Pour all ingredients (yes even the frozen chicken) into a Crock-Pot® and stir well. Put on low and allow to cook for 8 hours (the longer the better)!! When ready to serve remove chicken and shred with forks. Return chicken to slow cooker and mix well. If using an Instant Pot® pressure cooker, set to 'bean/chili' default setting, lock and seal lid, making sure vent is closed. Soup should be done cooking in 45 minutes to 1 hour. When cooking cycle finishes allow to sit for 15 minutes or so then release any remaining steam by opening vent. When ready to serve, remove chicken and shred with forks. Return chicken to pressure cooker and mix well. Serve with sour cream shredded cheddar cheese and crushed tortilla chips.

This recipe freezes very well ... if you have any leftovers, that is!!

SLOW COOKER CARNE GUISADA

Submitted by: Ariana Garcia

Prep time	Cook time	Serves
30-45 min	**6 hours (high)** **8 hours (low)**	**4-6**

- 2 pounds eye of round roast
- 1 teaspoon ground cumin
- 1 teaspoon garlic powder
- ½ teaspoon ground black pepper
- ½ teaspoon regular or seasoned salt
- 2 tablespoons tomato bouillon
- 6 ounces tomato sauce
- 7 ounces water

Flour Slurry:
- 3 tablespoons flour
- 5 ounces water

Turn on slow cooker to proper setting. Trim roast of any additional fat then cut into cubes about 1 inch in size and put in slow cooker. Add ground cumin, garlic powder, black pepper, salt, tomato bouillon, tomato sauce and 7 ounces water. Make a slurry with flour and 5 ounces water. Make sure there are no clumps of flour. Add to slow cooker. Mix ingredients making sure to combine well. Cook on high 4 to 6 hours or on low for 6 to 8 hours (the longer the meat cooks the softer and tender it will be). Serve with Mexican rice and refried beans or in a flour tortilla for tacos. Enjoy!

Growing up Hispanic, I loved all of the foods that my mother and grandmothers would make. I love Mexican food and thoroughly enjoy making it for my kids now. This recipe came about because I wanted something delicious that wouldn't have to be made on the stove for hours. This recipe is simple yet delicious.

BURRITO LASAGNA

Submitted by: Azure McDaniel

Prep time	Cook time	Serves
15 min	**30-35 min**	**12**

- 2 pounds ground beef
- 2 (10 oz) cans enchilada sauce
- 1 envelope taco seasoning
- 1 tablespoon cumin
- 1 (8.8 oz) package ready-to-serve Spanish rice
- 12 (8 in) flour tortillas, warmed
- 1 (15 oz) can refried beans
- 4 cups Mexican cheese blend, shredded

Optional Toppings:
- salsa
- sliced avocado
- shredded lettuce
- taco sauce
- sour cream

Preheat on oven to 350 degrees. In a large skillet, cook beef over medium heat until no longer pink, drain. Stir in enchilada sauce, taco seasoning and cumin, heat through. Heat Spanish rice according to package directions. Spread 1 cup meat mixture into a greased 13 x 9 baking dish. Layer with 4 tortillas and spread each tortilla with about 2 tablespoons refried beans, a third of the Spanish rice, a third of remaining meat mixture and a third of the cheese. Repeat layers. Top with remaining tortillas, Spanish rice and meat mixture (the dish will be full). Cover and bake at 350 degrees for 20 minutes. Sprinkle with the remaining cheese. Uncover, bake 10 to 15 minutes longer or until the cheese is melted. Let stand for 10 minutes before serving. Serve with the toppings of your choice.

SPAGHETTI PIE

Submitted by: Beth Burdick

Prep time	Cook time	Serves
15 min	**20-25 min**	**5-6**

- 6 ounces spaghetti noodles
- 2 tablespoon butter, melted
- 2 eggs, beaten
- $1/3$ cup parmesan cheese, grated
- $1/2$ pound ground beef
- 1 (14 oz) jar of spaghetti sauce
- $1/2$ cup mozzerella cheese, grated

Preheat oven to 350 degrees. Boil spaghetti, drain and cool. Brown ground beef, then stir in spaghetti sauce. Mix cooled noodles with butter, eggs and parmesan cheese. Press noodle mixture into greased 10-inch pie plate and form a nest. Spread meat mixture in the nest in the middle of noodles. Sprinkle with mozzerella cheese and bake for 20-25 minutes or until cheese is nicely brown.

This is a favorite childhood recipe that my mom would make often!! And it can be easily doubled, 1 for dinner and 1 for the freezer. If freezing, just be sure to completely thaw before baking & follow baking instructions in recipe.

HAMBURGER DELIGHT

Submitted by: Faith Lawrence

Prep time 10 min	Cook time 20 min	Serves 6-8

- 2 pounds hamburger
- 2 (15 oz) cans whole kernel corn
- 2 boxes beef vermicelli rice
- 4 tablespoon butter
- 2 cups water
- 1 small onion, diced

Put butter in a deep-dish pan (I use an iron Dutch oven). Add rice and packets of seasoning and brown.

Once browned, add the water. In a separate pan, fry hamburger and onions, add to rice with two cans corn. Cover and cook on medium heat, stirring occasionally.

Cook uncovered until liquids cook down.

I serve with bread and butter along with pepperoncini or olives. This is my youngest son, Matthew's favorite meal.

MARGIE'S
CHICKEN RICE PEAS

Submitted by: Joyce Keeler

Prep time 30 min	Cook time 25 min	Serves 4

- 1 to 2 chicken breasts, shredded or chopped
- ½ pound mild or hot sweet Italian sausage, cooked and crumbled
- 1 package Mahatma® Yellow Rice or white rice with saffron seasoning
- 1 cup frozen peas

Cook chicken to your liking (I generally put lots in a Crock-Pot® and shred and freeze for meals later). Fry sausage (if purchased as links remove casing. I generally cook a full pound and divide in half and freeze for two servings).

Thaw peas before cooking. Make rice according to directions. Cooking time is 20 minutes. About 15 minutes in, add meat and peas, stir and cook additional 5 to 8 minutes until done and serve. This is a very simple and forgiving recipe. You can add as much or as little meat and peas as desired. If you cook the chicken and sausage ahead of time like I do you just have to thaw while the rice is cooking and add at the end.

We always called this recipe CRP because until very recently my son didn't like sausage added. This recipe is from a good family friend. I began using the Mahatma® rice because saffron is so expensive to purchase. These packages are only ± $1 each. The recipe is very economical and doubles easily.

MEATLOAF

Submitted by: Christina Johns

Prep time 5-10 min	Cook time 1 hour and 10 min	Serves 10-12

- 2 pounds hamburger
- 1 package stuffing mix
  (I use Stove Top® Stuffing)
- 2 eggs
- 1 cup milk

Topping:
- 3 cups ketchup
- 1 cup brown sugar

Preheat oven to 350 degrees. In a large bowl, mix together hamburger, stuffing, eggs and milk. Next, grease a 9x13 pan. Add meatloaf mixture to greased pan. Grab a medium sized bowl and mix together 3 cups ketchup and 1 cup brown sugar. Then spread ketchup mixture over meatloaf mixture. Bake meatloaf for 1 hour and 10 minutes. It will come out perfect and so yummy.

I found that using a stuffing mix eliminates me from having to go around my kitchen looking for all the spices I need because they are all in the stuffing along with the bread. This is my family's favorite meal.

TATER TOT CASSEROLE

Submitted by: Angie Duerden

Prep time	Cook time	Serves
20 min	**40-45 min**	**10-12**

- 1 pound ground beef
- 1 (2 lb) bag frozen tater tots
- 1 (10.5 oz) can cream chicken soup
- 1 (10.5 oz) can cream celery soup
- 1 to 2 cups milk (or more if needed)
- 3 cups cheddar cheese, shredded
- dill weed
- garlic powder
- salt and pepper to taste

Preheat oven to 350 degrees. Brown ground beef, season with salt, pepper, garlic powder and dill weed. In a large bowl, add tater tots and ground beef, set aside. In a medium size bowl, add soup and 2 cups milk, then mix well. Pour soup mixture over tater tots and ground beef, mix well. Add 1 ½ cups shredded cheese reserving some for the top, mix well. Mixture should be a bit runny, so if it's too dry then add some more milk to thin it out. Place mixture in a 9x13 greased pan (just spray it with some cooking spray). Bake at 350 degrees, loosely covered, for 40 minutes and then the last 10 minutes take the cover off and add the rest of the cheese, bake until bubbly and the tots are brown on top. ENJOY!!

My family loves this meal, it's a feel good recipe. I feed this to approximately 100 girls and adults at our young women's camp each summer as one of their dinner meals.

TUNA POT PIE

Submitted by: Nancy Butler

Prep time	Cook time	Serves
20 min	40 min	4-6

- 2 boxes Pillsbury® refrigerated pie crusts (2 rolled crusts per box)
- 2 cans tuna fish
- 1 large bag frozen mixed vegetables
- 1 envelope Knorrs® vegetable soup
- 1 can cream of mushroom soup or cream of chicken soup
- 3 cups half and half or whole milk
- ¼ cup butter
- 4 tablespoon flour
- 1 teaspoon garlic powder
- salt and pepper to taste

Preheat oven to 425 degrees. Press 2 pie crusts into a 9 x 13 baking dish and bake at 425 degrees for 10 to 12 minutes. In large pan, melt butter and add flour to make a roux. Add milk and soup and cook till thick. Add remaining ingredients (don't drain tuna) and mix well. Pour into baked shell and add 2 more crusts to top and pinch edges together. Bake at 425 degrees for 30 minutes.

I think of the Christmas episode when they were trying to come up with food for the Christmas banquet and all they had was a bunch of fish. This recipe could have worked. Now everytime I make it I think of this Christmas episode in Hope Valley. I have made it for years.

HAM AND CHEESE BRUNCH SANDWICH

Submitted by: Marsha Etzrodt

Prep time	Cook time	Serves
30 min	45 min	8

Ingredients

- 16 slices sandwich bread
- 8 slices sharp cheese
- 8 slices boiled ham
- 6 eggs
- 3 cups milk
- ½ teaspoon dry mustard
- 1 small can mushrooms
- 1 cup cornflakes, crushed
- ½ cup butter, melted
- butter for buttering bread

Instructions

Cut crusts from the bread, butter one side. Place 8 slices of buttered bread (buttered side down) in well-greased 13 x 9 baking dish. Top each slice with ham and cheese.

Put the other 8 buttered slices of bread on top, buttered side up. In medium bowl, mix eggs, milk and dry mustard. Pour over all bread. Refrigerate overnight.

Preheat oven to 350 degrees. Place mushrooms on top of bread. Then sprinkle cornflakes with melted butter on top of all.

Bake 45 minutes at 350 degrees.

Notes

This recipe is a family favorite.

ONE PAN BREAKFAST

Submitted by: Bethany Lewton

Prep time	Cook time	Serves
35 min	**65 min**	**7-10**

- 4 to 5 large potatoes
- 1 medium onion, chopped
- 1 cup cooked ham, chopped
- 16 cherry tomatoes, sliced
- 12 ounces Velveeta®, cubed
- 1 cup milk
- 12 eggs

Preheat oven to 350 degrees. Slice potatoes thin (1/8 inch thick) and overlap in a 9 x 13 glass pan. Place pan in oven for 11 minutes. Remove from oven and place on cooling rack. Then preheat oven to 400 degrees. Layer onion, ham and tomatoes on top of potatoes. Crack eggs in bowl, add milk and cubed Velveeta®, then whisk (can be a little chunky). Pour on top of potato mixture. Cook 45 minutes. Take pan out of oven, cover with tin foil and cook for 20 minutes. Mixture should be set and golden brown on top. Remove from oven and serve warm. Enjoy!

I made up this recipe when I was making lunch for my family. It was a hit! We like to serve it with blueberry muffins.

OVEN BAKED DENVER OMELET

Submitted by: Debbie Wesselius

Prep time	Cook time	Serves
15 min	**30 min**	**4**

- 8 eggs
- ½ cup half and half cream
- 1 cup cheddar cheese, shredded
- 1 cup fully cooked ham, chopped
- ½ cup onion
- ½ cup green pepper

Preheat oven to 400 degrees. In a medium sized mixing bowl, whisk together eggs and cream.

Add in cheese, ham, onion and green pepper. Pour into a greased 9x9 inch pan.

Bake for 25 minutes or until golden brown.

My family loves this for breakfast. So quick and easy.

SAUSAGE EGG CASSEROLE

Submitted by: Pam Calhoon

Prep time **15 min**	Cook time **40 min**	Serves **6**

- 1 pound bulk sausage
- 6 eggs
- 2 cups fresh bread cubes
- 2 cups milk
- 1 cup cheddar cheese, shredded
- ½ teaspoon dry mustard

Preheat oven to 350 degrees. Cook sausage and drain well. In a large bowl, combine eggs, milk and dry mustard then stir with a whisk until well mixed. Add bread cubes, cheese, sausage and mix well. Pour ingredients into greased

casserole dish (at this point you can cover it and refrigerate overnight if you wish). Bake in preheated oven at 350 degrees for 40 minutes or until a knife inserted in the middle comes out clean (if refrigerated overnight may take a bit longer to cook).

This is a great holiday breakfast as you can make it the night before. It easily doubles or triples. Serve with fruit and muffins or favorite breakfast roll. This has been a family favorite since I was a child.

CRUSTLESS ASPARAGUS AND HAM QUICHE

Submitted by: Judy Mulder

Prep time	Cook time	Serves
30 min	**30 min**	**6-8**

- 1 tablespoon olive oil
- 1 tablespoon butter
- 1 leek, thinly sliced
- ½ pound asparagus, cut into 1 inch pieces
- 1 cup grated Gruyere cheese (or Swiss cheese)
- 8 ounces ham, cubed
- 6 large eggs
- 1 cup heavy cream
- salt and pepper to taste

Preheat oven to 400 degrees. Spray a 9 or 10 inch pie plate with coconut oil. Heat a large skillet over medium heat. Add olive oil and butter. When butter is melted, add leek, asparagus pieces and cook until tender (8 to10 minutes). Then add ham and continue to cook until heated through. Scrape mixture into pie plate. Top with grated cheese. In a medium bowl, whisk together eggs, cream, salt and pepper. Pour over the ingredients in the pie plate. Bake 30 minutes or until knife inserted into center comes out clean.

GINGERBREAD PANCAKES

Submitted by: Pat Cory

Prep time	Cook time	Serves
15 min	**6-8 min**	**8 pancakes**

- 1 ½ cups all-purpose flour
- 2 teaspoons baking powder
- ½ teaspoon baking soda
- ½ teaspoon salt
- 2 teaspoons ground ginger
- 2 teaspoons ground cinnamon
- 1 teaspoon ground cloves
- 2 eggs
- ¼ cup brown sugar, firmly packed
- 1 cup buttermilk (I use sour milk made with 1 tablespoon vinegar to 1 cup milk)
- 2 tablespoons molasses
- 4 tablespoons butter, melted and cooled
- ½ cup water

Whisk first 7 ingredients together in one bowl. In second bowl, beat eggs and brown sugar with a wire whisk. Beat in buttermilk, molasses, cooled butter and ½ cup water. Then add flour mixture and beat once or twice until almost smooth (don't overwork mixture, a few lumps are good). Cook like you would any other pancakes.

Wonderful for a special breakfast or a warm cozy dinner on a cold winter day.

BRIOCHE FRENCH TOAST

Submitted by: Jeff McGee

Prep time	Cook time	Serves
15 min	**20 min**	**4**

- 4 eggs
- ¾ cup milk
- 2 tablespoons sugar
- 1 teaspoon ground cinnamon
- 8 slices thick brioche bread (or any choice)
- butter (for cooking)
- confectioners' sugar (for garnish)

Fruit Compote:
- 4 peaches
- 1 (1 lb) container strawberries
- 2 (6 oz) containers blueberries
- ¼ water
- ¼ cup maple syrup (pure organic)

Maple Whipped Cream:
- 1 cup heavy whipping cream
- 4 tablespoons maple syrup (pure organic)

Peel and dice peaches, then cut off stem of strawberries and cut in half. In a medium size pot, add all fruit, ¼ cup water and ¼ cup maple syrup. Cook for 20 minutes on medium, then set aside. Next, in a bowl mix eggs, milk, cinnamon and sugar together. Whisk until well blended and pour into a shallow bowl. Then dip each slice of bread into the egg mixture, allowing bread to soak up some of the mixture. Melt butter over a large skillet on medium high heat. Add as many slices of bread onto the skillet as will fit at a time. Fry until browned, flipping the bread when golden on each side. While cooking, use a mixer to whip 1 cup cream until stiff and then fold in 4 tablespoons maple syrup. Serve French toast with fruit compote, maple syrup whipped cream and dust with confetioners' sugar.

A family favorite!

MAPLE CINNAMON COLD CEREAL

Submitted by: Karen French

Prep time	Cook time	Serves
24 hours	**30 min**	**20**

- 6 cups flour (freshly ground is optimal for nutrition) I use a mixture of almond and oat flour
- 3 cups whole plain yogurt
- ¾ cup coconut oil
- 1 cup pure maple syrup (you can substitute part of this out for a sweetener such as stevia)
- 2 teaspoon baking soda
- 1 teaspoon vanilla
- 1 teaspoon maple extract
- 1 teaspoon sea salt
- 1 tablespoon cinnamon
- Protein Powder (optional)

Mix the flour and yogurt in a large glass bowl. Cover with a clean cloth and let it sit on the counter for 24 hours. Preheat the oven to 350 degrees. Mix all the remaining ingredients into the batter. Pour into two 9x13 pans and bake for 30 minutes or until a toothpick inserted comes out clean. Do not over bake! Let it cool and crumble the cake into small chunks/crumbs. I prefer the pieces to be small but many like them to be about the size of a dime. Preheat the oven to 200 degrees.

Place crumbs back in pans, put in oven to dehydrate for about 12-18 hours turning the cereal every few hours to dry evenly. This may take less time if you crumble the pieces really small.

Once it's dry serve with milk; or it's great as a dry snack or on yogurt!

DESSERTS

ANOTHER HEARTIE HELPING

CHOCOLATE PEANUTBUTTER BARS

Submitted by: Barbara J. Laird

Prep time	Cook time	Serves
30 min	**None**	**24 bars**

- 1 cup peanut butter (I like the chunky)
- 1 cup margarine
- 1 cup graham cracker crumbs
- 1 pound confectioners' sugar
- 1 (12 oz) bag semi-sweet chocolate chips

Melt margarine in the microwave and cool. In a separate bowl, mix graham cracker crumbs, confectioners' sugar and peanut butter (can mix with a fork). Add melted margarine and mix to combine. Put mixture in a 13 x 9 inch pan that has been greased with solid margarine. Pat mixture down to fit pan. Melt chocolate chips in microwave.

Spread evenly on top of peanut butter mixture. Refrigerate 15 minutes. Remove from refrigerator and cut into 24 squares. Return to refrigerator and store covered.

If you can count to one you can make this recipe. I have been making these since my boys were small. I would give my son one in his lunch for school. The next day he would ask for two, then three, and more each day. It turned out he was selling them to his friends for 50 cents each! These are a big hit at my church bake sale.

LOADED RICE KRISPIE® TREATS

Submitted by: Lori Meeker

Prep time	Cook time	Serves
20 min	**4 min**	**20-25**

ingredients

- ¼ cup butter (or margarine)
- 1 (10 oz) bag mini marshmallows
- ½ cup peanut butter (smooth or chunky)
- 5 cups Rice Krispie® cereal (generic works fine)
- 1 cup M&M's® (plain peanut or your favorite flavor)
- 1 cup butterscotch chips
- 2 cups semisweet chocolate chips

instructions

Prepare a 9 x 13 cake pan with non-stick cooking spray. In a large glass bowl, melt ¼ cup butter (or margarine) in the microwave. Add marshmallows to butter and stir. Microwave for about 2 minutes or until marshmallows are puffy and easy to stir. Add ½ cup peanut butter to butter and marshmallow mixture, stir to blend. Add Rice Krispies® and M&M's® and stir. Put into 9 x 13 cake pan. Spread out evenly. In another bowl, melt butterscotch and chocolate chips together for 2 minutes. Let sit about 5 minutes then stir until smooth. Pour mixture over Rice Krispies® treats and spread evenly over top. Cool in the fridge so top layer will harden. Cut and serve. You may want to let it stand at room temperature for a few minutes to make cutting easier.

notes

Easy and yummy! Recipe was shared with me in 1991 when my son was born, and it's one of his favorites!

S'MOORE BARS

Submitted by: Beth A Tunny

Prep time	Cook time	Serves
30 min	**20 min**	**10-12**

- ¾ cup butter, softened
- ⅔ cup sugar
- 1 egg
- 1 teaspoon vanilla extract
- 3 cups graham cracker crumbs
- ½ cup all-purpose flour
- ½ teaspoon salt
- 8 to 9 Hershey's® bars
- 3 cups miniature marshmallows

Preheat oven to 325 degrees. Grease a 9x13 inch dish. In a large bowl, beat butter. Add sugar and beat on medium speed until light and fluffy. Blend in egg and vanilla. Stir in graham cracker crumbs, flour and salt. Set aside 1 ½ to 2 cups of mixture. Press remaining mixture into bottom of prepared dish. Break chocolate bars into small pieces and spread onto crumb mixture. Sprinkle marshmallows evenly on top of chocolate. Crumble reserved mixture on top of the marshmallows. Bake 20 to 25 minutes but watch the marshmallows. You don't want them too brown, just lightly brown. Cool for 10 minutes, then cut and try not to eat them because they are delicious!

I got this recipe from a neighbor and they are hands down the best. The combination of the chocolate, marshmallows and the crumb is just too good. Never any left. Great for parties, bringing to someone's house as a gift or just feel like making something really good. Plus they are great year round. Everyone always asks for the recipe. It's a keeper.

HOPE VALLEY'S SECRET FUDGE

Submitted by: Robyn Barstad

Prep time	Cook time	Serves
about 20 min	**5 min**	**6-8**

- 1 small package semi-sweet chocolate chips
- 1 small package butterscotch chips
- ½ cup crunchy peanut butter
- 5 cups cornflakes

Melt first 3 ingredients in double boiler stirring constantly. Pour 5 cups cornflakes into large bowl. When the chocolate chips, butterscotch chips and peanut butter have melted together, pour over the cornflakes in bowl and stir to blend. Pour mixture into square pan. Set the fudge in refrigerator, but not too long (½ hour). Bring out and cut in squares.

Do make sure not to leave the fudge in refrigerator too long, it will make it hard to cut. Always take this to pot lucks and make it at Christmas time. People are always wondering what is in the fudge, some never guess it is cornflakes!! It has been in our family for a long time. The kids love it. They nick named it, Santa Fudge at Christmas.

SPICE DROPS

Submitted by: Janet Idziak

Prep time	Cook time	Serves
10-15 min	**10-12 min**	**36 cookies**

- 6 tablespoons butter (margarine)
- ¼ cup granulated sugar
- ¼ cup brown sugar
- ½ teaspoon vanilla
- 1 egg
- 1 cup flour, sifted
- 1 teaspoon baking powder
- ½ teaspoon salt
- 1 teaspoon cinnamon
- ½ teaspoon allspice
- ¼ teaspoon ground cloves
- ¼ teaspoon nutmeg
- ½ cup nuts, chopped
- ½ cup chocolate bits or chips
- 2 tablespoons milk

Preheat oven to 375 degrees. Cream butter (or margarine), two sugars and vanilla. Beat until fluffy adding egg. Sift together flour, baking powder, salt and spices in a separate bowl. Then stir in nuts and chocolate until lightly covered. Combine two mixtures adding milk. Stir until blended. Drop with teaspoon on greased cookie sheets. Bake in oven 375 degrees for 10 to 12 minutes.

Grandma Elsie's recipe, at least 50 years old but probably older.

ALLERGEN FREE SOFT DELICIOUS
CHOCOLATE CHIP COOKIES

Submitted by: Sarah Storm

Prep time	Cook time	Serves
12 min	**10 min**	**24 Cookies**

- ¼ cup dark chocolate chips allergen free (Enjoy Life® brand or other varieties)
- ¼ cup palm shortening
- 1 egg, room temperature
- ¼ cup coconut crystals
- 2 tablespoons honey
- 2 teaspoons vanilla extract
- 1 ½ cups almond flour
- 2 teaspoons coconut flour
- ½ teaspoon baking soda
- ½ teaspoon salt
- parchment paper for cookie sheets

Preheat oven to 325 degrees. Mix all wet ingredient to get it creamy, for softness of cookies. Mix dry ingredients separately to get out clumps. Then in a bowl, combine all ingredients and mix together. Finally add in chocolate chips and stir. Use a 1 tablespoon scoop to scoop cookie dough and put on parchment paper for best results. Enjoy! Milk free, gluten free, and sugar free.

This recipe has been tweaked and made several times as a result of severe food allergies to be able to eat delicious chocolate chip cookies.

CHOCOLATE MINT BROWNIES

Submitted by: Holly Hall

Prep time	Cook time	Serves
1-3 hours	**20 min**	**6-8**

- ½ cup butter, melted
- 1 cup sugar
- 4 eggs
- 1 cup flour
- 1 (16 oz) bottle Hershey's® Syrup
- 1 teaspoon vanilla extract

Filling:
- ½ cup butter, melted
- 3 cups powdered sugar
- ¼ cup cream
- 5 to 6 drops of green food coloring
- 1 teaspoon peppermint extract

Topping:
- ¼ cup butter
- 1 (6 oz) bag chocolate chips

Preheat oven to 350 degrees. Cream butter and sugar together. Add eggs one at a time. Add flour, Hershey's® syrup and vanilla extract. Spread in a greased 17x11 inch pan. Bake at 350 degrees for 20 minutes. Cool. For the filling, cream all filling ingredients together. Spread on cooled brownie and refrigerate. For the topping, melt ingredients together, spread on filling and refrigerate again.

I first came across this brownie at a local library in Post Falls, Idaho in 1999. It instantly became one of my favorites. My method is to melt the butter to make mixing the ingredients easier and allow each layer to cool before you add the next one. It is a favorite in this household and is delicious with coffee, tea, and milk. Every time I make it for family and friends, it is an instant hit.

PUMPKIN SPICE HOT CHOCOLATE CUPCAKES

Submitted by: Vanessa Sawyer

Prep time	Cook time	Serves
15 min	**20 min**	**12**

- ½ cup oil or butter
- ¼ cup cocoa
- 1 ¼ cup cake flour
- 1 teaspoon baking soda
- 1 teaspoon baking powder
- 2 eggs
- ¼ cup pumpkin spiced hot chocolate mix
- ¼ cup sugar
- ½ cup milk

Frosting:
- 8 ounces cream cheese
- 7 to 8 ounces marshmallow cream
- ½ cup confectioners' sugar
- ¼ cup pumpkin spiced hot chocolate mix
- mini marshmallows for topping

Preheat oven to 350 degrees. In a medium bowl, combine oil, cocoa, cake flour, baking soda, baking powder, eggs, hot chocolate mix, sugar and milk. Mix together with a hand mixer until thoroughly combine. Pour batter into cupcake liners. Fill each wrapper about ⅔ full. Bake for about 18 to 20 minutes. Place on a cooling rack to cool completely. While cooling, mix together cream cheese, marshmallow cream, confectioners' sugar and hot chocolate mix with a hand or stand mixer, thoroughly combine. Place mixture into a pastry bag with your favorite decorator tip on the end. Decorate cupcakes by swirling icing from the inside center to the outside. Sprinkle with mini marshmallows. Optional: insert ½ a paper straw into each cupcake.

You can make your own pumpkin spice hot chocolate by adding ¼ teaspoon cinnamon, ¼ teaspoon ground ginger, ¼ teaspoon nutmeg, and ¼ teaspoon of pumpkin pie spice. Or you can use regular hot chocolate mix. If your icing is too thick add a little bit of heavy cream at a time for desired consistency.

CARROT CAKE WITH CREAM CHEESE ICING

Submitted by: Courtney Manasco

Prep time	Cook time	Serves
45 min	**35 min**	**24**

- 2 cups all-purpose flour
- 2 cups sugar
- 2 teaspoons salt
- 2 teaspoons baking soda
- 2 teaspoons cinnamon
- 4 large eggs
- 1 ½ cups cooking oil (or to preferred consistency)
- 3 cups carrots, finely grated

Icing:
- ½ cup butter (or margarine)
- 8 ounces cream cheese
- 1 (1 lb) box powdered sugar
- 1 cup pecans
- ½ tablespoon vanilla extract

Preheat oven to 350 degrees. Mix all dry ingredients (flour, sugar, salt, soda, cinnamon) and add one egg at a time, beaten. Add cooking oil and carrots; mix well. Line two cake pans with wax paper and flour to avoid sticking. Divide cake mix evenly between cake pans. Bake for 35 minutes or until cake is done in the middle of each pan. While cake bakes, mix together icing ingredients. Set aside until cake is baked and cooled before icing. (Lick the icing bowl until clean and when cake is iced) ENJOY!

My Mom isn't sure exactly which Aunt it came from, but has been in the family since the 30's. It has been a favorite of many generations of family and friends. I think the cream cheese icing is the draw....along with no raisins.

TO DIE FOR GERMAN CHOCOLATE CAKE

Submitted by: Luanne Maroney

Prep time	Cook time	Serves
15-20 min	**30-40 min**	**12-14**

ingredients

- 1 (4 oz) package Baker's® German chocolate bar
- ½ cup boiling water
- 1 cup margarine
- 2 cups sugar
- 4 egg yolks
- 2 cups granulated sugar
- 1 cup buttermilk
- 1 teaspoon vanilla extract
- 1 teaspoon baking soda
- ½ teaspoon salt
- 2 ½ cup all-purpose flour
- 4 egg whites, stiffly beaten

instructions

Preheat oven to 350 degrees. Melt chocolate bars in boiling water in small mixing bowl. Cream margarine and sugar together, in large mixing bowl, until fluffy. Add egg yolks (saving the whites) one at a time and mix into sugar and margarine mixture. Now add vanilla and melted chocolate mixture. Sift flour with soda and salt in separate bowl, add to wet mixture alternating with buttermilk. Beat egg whites until stiff and fluffy. Fold egg whites into cake mixture last. Pour into 3 greased and floured 8 inch or 9 inch cake pans. Bake 30 to 40 minutes. Check with toothpick. If clean, remove and cool 10 to 15 minutes. Remove from pans to cooling racks before icing.

notes

This recipe is a favorite of my mother's and one I ALWAYS requested for my birthday every year in July. It is rich and moist and has a "to die for" flavor if you love chocolate, coconut and pecans! Since my birthday is in July, we always had my mother's homemade vanilla custard style ice cream with this, which made it all the more special!!! I could see Abigail serving this in her cafe or bringing it to an ice cream social.

CHOCOLATE CANDY BAR CAKE

Submitted by: Sonya Williams

Prep time 15 min	Cook time 16-20 min	Serves 12-16

- 1 box Swiss chocolate cake mix
- ¾ cup vegetable oil
- 1 ½ cups milk
- 1 small package instant vanilla pudding
- 3 eggs

Icing:

- 1 (8 oz) package cream cheese, softened
- 1 cup sugar
- 1 ½ cups powdered sugar
- 6 chocolate candy bars, chopped (1.55 oz. each)
- 1 (12 oz) container Cool Whip®

Preheat oven to 350 degrees. Spray three 9 inch cake pans with cooking spray and set aside. Mix cake mix, oil, milk, vanilla pudding and eggs in a large mixing bowl on low for one minute until blended. Then mix for two minutes on medium high until smooth. Pour into three 9 inch cake pans and bake for 16 to 20 minutes (or until inserted toothpick comes out clean) in 350 degree oven. Cool cakes until room temperature before frosting. For the icing, cream together cream cheese, sugar and powdered sugar in a large mixing bowl on medium high until well blended. Fold in four of the chopped candy bars and Cool Whip®, saving two candy bars for garnishing after frosting. Frost and stack the cooled cake layers using the remaining two chopped candy bars to garnish on top and sides after frosting.

I use Hershey's® candy bars for this recipe.

CHOCOLATE CHIP POUND CAKE

Submitted by: Caitlin Floyd

Prep time	Cook time	Serves
10 min	**1 hour**	**10-12**

ingredients

- 1 box yellow cake mix
- 2 (4 oz) boxes chocolate instant pudding mix
- ½ cup oil
- 1 ½ cups water
- 4 large eggs
- 1 to 1 ½ cups chocolate chips

instructions

Preheat oven to 325 degrees. Grease down Bundt® pan well with butter, shortening or cooking spray. Mix all ingredients except chocolate chips until smooth. Then stir in chocolate chips. Pour batter into pan evenly. Bake for 1 hour or until toothpick comes out clean.

notes

Family favorite and so easy to make!

PINEAPPLE SHEET CAKE

Submitted by: Barb Kenady

Prep time	Cook time	Serves
15 min	**35 min**	**30**

- 2 cups all-purpose flour
- 2 cups sugar
- 2 large eggs
- 1 cup nuts, chopped
- 2 teaspoon baking soda
- ½ teaspoon salt
- 1 teaspoon vanilla extract
- 1 (20 oz) can crushed pineapple, undrained

Icing:
- 1 (8 oz) cream cheese, softened
- ½ cup butter, softened
- 3 ¾ cup powdered sugar
- 1 teaspoon vanilla extract
- ½ cup nuts, chopped

Preheat oven to 350 degrees. In large bowl, combine all cake ingredients and beat until smooth. Pour into a greased 15x10x1 inch baking pan. Bake at 350 degrees for 35 minutes, then cool. For icing, in a small bowl, combine all the icing ingredients. Beat until smooth. Spread over cake. Sprinkle with nuts (optional).

This is a dessert that I take to family reunions, church pot lucks etc. Very rarely any leftovers to take home!! Travels well.

WALDORF RED VELVET CAKE

Submitted by: Kim Johnson

Prep time	Cook time	Serves
30 min	**30-40 min**	**8**

ingredients

- ½ cup Crisco®
- 1 ½ cups white sugar
- 2 eggs
- ¼ cup red food coloring
- 2 teaspoon cocoa
- 1 teaspoon vanilla
- 1 teaspoon salt
- 1 cup buttermilk
- 2 ½ cups flour
- 1 teaspoon vinegar
- 1 teaspoon baking soda

instructions

Preheat oven to 350 degrees. Cream Crisco® and sugar together and then add eggs one at a time. Beat 1 minute. In a separate bowl, mix cocoa and food coloring together and make a paste. Add to egg mixture. In a small bowl, mix salt, vanilla and buttermilk. Add to egg mixture. In another bowl, mix vinegar and baking soda. Add to mixture. Blend until mixed. Pour into greased 9 inch round pans and bake for 30 to 40 minutes. Cool for 5 minutes and remove from pans. Once completely cooled ice with a cream cheese icing.

notes

My Grandma Steele got this recipe from the Waldorf Astoria Hotel in New York when she and my Grandfather were there for one of their anniversaries. Grandma used to make it at Christmas and now I make it at Christmas. It is one of the many good memories I have of my Grandma.

PINK LEMONADE PIE

Submitted by: Carol Lee Cherry

Prep time	Cook time	Serves
15 min	**None**	**6-12**

- 2 premade graham cracker crusts (or chocolate crusts)
- 1 (12 oz) can pink or regular frozen lemonade mix, thawed
- 1 (14 oz) can condensed milk (<u>not</u> evaporated milk)
- 1 (16 oz) container frozen whipped topping, thawed (like Cool Whip®)

Optional:
- red food coloring
- strawberries or raspberries

Thaw frozen lemonade and whipped topping in refrigerator overnight. Do not mix the lemonade with water. In a large bowl, combine condensed milk, thawed lemonade and mix well. If desired, add several drops of red food coloring to enhance the color. Add whipped topping to mixture and mix well but avoid beating too much. It will begin to set up so mixture needs to be poured into the pie crusts quickly. Smooth filling in both crusts or if using one crust use the back of a spoon to whip up the filling into small peaks. Decorate with fresh raspberries or sliced strawberries. Enjoy!

I've been making this pie since 1974. Quick and easy especially if you forget you need something for a potluck. So rich that you need to cut thin slices which can result in 8 or more slices per pie.

The recipe makes 2 pies or for spectacular pie, mound all into one pie! Chocolate crust makes for a wonderful pie!

MOM'S PUMPKIN PIE

Submitted by: Eriikka Kopycinski

Prep time	Cook time	Serves
25 min	**40-45 min**	**8**

ingredients

- 1 ½ cups pumpkin (1 can)
- 1 cup brown sugar (light)
- ½ teaspoon salt
- 2 teaspoon cinnamon
- 1 teaspoon ginger
- 2 tablespoons molasses
- 3 eggs, beaten
- 1 cup evaporated milk
- 1 pie crust

instructions

Preheat oven to 425 degrees. Combine the first six ingredients. Add eggs and milk, (one small can of evaporated milk makes ¾ cups. Just fill the rest of the cup with water) mix thoroughly. Pour into your own or ready-made pie shell. Bake 40 to 45 minutes or until the middle is set. The recipe is a favorite in our household.

notes

This is my mother's recipe since the 50's, I still have the original recipe she wrote out.

This is a dessert the family looks forward to every Thanksgiving and I make two!

I use the ¼ cup of water to make up the cup of evaporated milk every time I make this recipe and pies turn out delicious.

BANANA CREAM PIE

Submitted by: Heather Kauffold

Prep time	Cook time	Serves
30 mins.	**11-15 min**	**8-10**

Pie Crust:

- 1 cup flour
- 1 cup walnuts, or pecans, diced
- ½ cup butter, melted
- or 1 premade pie crust

Pie Filling:

- 8 ounces cream cheese, softened
- 1 cup powdered sugar
- 2 (8 oz) containers Cool Whip®
- 2 (3 oz) boxes instant banana pudding
- 3 cups milk
- 3 bananas

Preheat oven 350 degrees.

<u>Crust:</u> In a mixing bowl add flour, walnuts and butter, mix until blended. Pour into pie container and press mix all over bottom and sides of pie tin, thin even layer. Bake for 11 to 15 minutes. Set aside to cool or I put it in the freezer to cool while I am making the next layer.

<u>Filling:</u> In a mixing bowl, combine cream cheese, powdered sugar and 8 ounces Cool Whip®. Mix until well blended about 5 mins. With a spatula, spread pie filling over top of pie crust then set it aside. Next, in a mixing bowl, combine pudding, milk and mix well. Once done mixing, quickly pour into pie container. Peel and cut bananas into thin slices then layer on top of pudding in the pie tin spaced however you choose.

For the topping, spread remaining Cool Whip® over the top of the pie. Cover all the bananas then sprinkle some diced walnuts. Eat right away or put in the fridge to chill for later.

I got this recipe from my cousin Sandy about 12 years ago and everyone in my family loves it. Whenever we have a get together I am asked to make it.

APPLE PUDDING WITH WARM VANILLA SAUCE

Submitted by: Nancy Butler

Prep time	Cook time	Serves
30 min	**45 min**	**8**

Ingredients

- 1 cup sugar
- ¼ cup butter, softened
- 1 egg
- 1 cup flour
- 1 teaspoon baking soda
- 1 ½ teaspoon cinnamon
- 1 teaspoon nutmeg
- ½ cup nut meats (optional)
- 4 peeled apples, diced

Vanilla Sauce:

- ½ cup butter
- 1 cup sugar
- 2 tablespoons flour
- 1 cup half and half
- 1 teaspoon vanilla

Instructions

Preheat oven to 350 degrees. Mix all ingredients well, except apples, with mixer. Stir in apples and pour into greased and floured 8 x 6 glass baking dish. Bake for 45 minutes. For the vanilla sauce, melt butter in sauce pan. Mix flour and sugar well and add to melted butter, stir well. Add half and half and bring just to a boil. Reduce heat to low and cook till thick watching carefully. When thickened remove from heat and stir in vanilla. Serve warm over apple pudding slices.

Notes

This recipe has been in our family for a long time. Everytime I see the ladies of Hope Valley having tea, I think of this recipe. It is so good served with a hot cup of tea.

STRAWBERRY SHORTCAKE

Submitted by: Judy Mulder

Prep time	Cook time	Serves
20 min	**15 min**	**6-9**

- 1 ½ cups flour
- 3 tablespoons sugar
- 2 ½ teaspoons baking powder
- ½ teaspoon salt
- ½ cup butter
- 1 large egg, beaten
- ½ cup milk
- strawberries
- sugar to taste
- whipped cream

Preheat oven to 450 degrees. Wash strawberries, remove stems, chop and place in bowl and sweeten to taste. In another bowl add flour, sugar, baking powder and salt, mix. Slice butter and add to dry ingredients. Cut in using two knives, as you would for a pie crust, until you have pea-size pieces of butter. Add egg to ½ cup milk and mix well. Add liquid to dry ingredients and butter, then mix (batter will be thick). Spread in a 9x9 pan and bake for 15 minutes or until top is golden.

Serve warm topped with strawberries and whipped cream, if desired. (You can double recipe for a 9x13 pan or use a pie pan).

My mom made this recipe every year when the strawberries were ripe. It brings back wonderful memories whenever I make and serve it.

QUICK COOKING NEW ZEALAND (KIWI) PAVLOVA

Submitted by: Angela Bycroft

Prep time	Cook time	Serves
15 min	**35 min**	**4-6**

- 2 ½ cups caster sugar (powdered sugar)
- 1 dessert spoon (or 2 teaspoons) corn flour
- 4 tablespoons boiling water
- 1 teaspoon vinegar
- 1 teaspoon vanilla essence (extract)
- 3 egg whites

Toppings:
- whipped cream
- berries and kiwi

Preheat oven to 300 degrees. Put all ingredients into a bowl and beat well until stiff. Place on tin foil sprinkled with sugar or onto an oven proof serving dish. Cook at 300 degrees for 35 minutes. Once done, let cool (ideally) completely or remove and cool if in a hurry (may collapse a little but still tastes amazing). Decorate with fresh berries, kiwi fruit and whipped cream. If left without cream, can be used following day.

Classic NZ dessert. Debate rages between Australia and NZ as to who actually invented the classic Pavlova but we mantain it was New Zealand. Always popular especially at Christmas time as it's the hottest month in the southern hemisphere.

RECIPE INDEX

Special Thanks to

Chef Jeff McGee and our Bakers:

René Wallach
Shelley Moss
Carrie Lengl
Jessica Frangione